3D Rendering in Windows®

How to display three-dimensional objects in Windows® with and without OpenGL®

by D. James Benton

Preface

This is a how-to guide on rendering three-dimensional objects. The target operating system is Windows®, but these same principles and techniques could be used in other contexts. The primary implementation is based on OpenGL®, but alternate rendering systems are also presented.

There are several obstacles for the developer to overcome in order to use OpenGL® on the Windows® operating system. The Microsoft® C compiler will no longer build the examples originally provided by Silicon Graphics® without modifications. I have fixed scores of them. They can be downloaded from my web site.

Microsoft® supported–even promoted–OpenGL® before their own system, DirectX®, provided 3D rendering. Microsoft® currently tolerates the existence of OpenGL®, much like they tolerate the existence of Apple® computers and Linux®. They do nothing to facilitate support and have made more than enough changes to their C compiler to frustrate all but the most persistent developers.

The creators of OpenGL®, Silicon Graphics, Inc., filed for bankruptcy in 2009. There is no longer an official OpenGL® SDK, but there is an extensive and fiercely loyal user and support community, so that OpenGL® will persist for a long time to come. The video graphics hardware developers are heavily invested in the survival of OpenGL®, as Microsoft® controls DirectX®.

All of the examples contained in this book,
(as well as a lot of free programs) are available at...

https://www.dudleybenton.altervista.org/software/index.html

i

Table of Contents

Introduction

There are many books and articles on rendering 3D objects using OpenGL®. This is intended as a supplement to, not a replacement for, such texts. The problem with most references is that they leave out a lot of essential information in some areas and overwhelm you with too much information in others. For instance, there may be a dozen ways of doing the same thing. Only one is necessary–but which one?

OpenGL® is very powerful, but it has certain limitations. There are two reasons you might want to render 3D objects without this powerful library: 1) it isn't compatible with your system and 2) you don't want to be locked into 24-bit color depth. OpenGL® and 24-bits/pixel are inseparable: you don't get one without the other. Several methods for rendering 3D images are presented in this book. Fully functioning codes and libraries are provided on line for every example, including the T-Rex depicted on the cover.

3D rendering is an important part of graphical user interface design, data analysis and presentation, game design, prototype design, and marketing. There are many tools available for 3D rendering–ranging from free to very expensive. Such tools can be used to build static content that can be played back through your application. Live rendering in response to user input is far preferable and can be built into your application with a reasonable level of effort. There are over fifty complete examples provided with this book that will help you do just that.

Chapter 1. Basic Concepts

There are eight basic considerations in creating and displaying a three-dimensional scene:

1) The relationship between the viewer and the scene (the view).
2) The coordinate transformations (the math).
3) The geometric representation of the scene (the objects).
4) The type and position of the light sources (the lighting).
5) How the surface of the objects reacts to lighting (shading, scattering, & reflecting).
6) Modifying light/object interactions (shadows & stenciling).
7) Combining the elements above to create the scene (rendering).
8) Displaying the rendered scene (painting).

There are also eight steps to implement these in a Windows® program:

1) Load the resources (bitmaps, icons, meshes, etc.).
2) Register the classes[1] (the main window plus any special controls).
3) Create the windows (the main window plus any special controls).
4) Establish the context[2] for rendering.
5) Gather user inputs (angles and distance between viewer and objects, determine which objects will be included, position of light source, etc.).
6) Render the scene.
7) Paint the rendering onto the display.
8) Check for user input and return to step 5.

We will cover each of these in the subsequent chapters. We will first consider rendering with the OpenGL® system and then with an alternate one.

---

[1] Note that Windows® classes have nothing to do with classes in C++.
[2] Device contexts and pixel formats will be discussed later.

3

Chapter 2. The View

The relationship between the viewer and the scene is illustrated in the following figure:

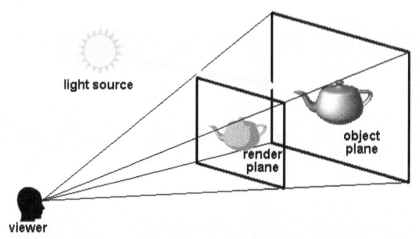

The light shines from the source onto the object. The surface of the object reacts to the light. Modified light then travels from the object to the viewer, passing through the render plane. Our goal is to construct what would appear in the render plane and paint this on the display.

If the render plane is closer to the viewer than to the object, there will be no perception of depth. When this distance goes to zero, the orthographic projection results. As the render plane gets closer to the object than to the viewer, the perception of depth will be exaggerated. A rendering that preserves the perception of depth as illustrated above is called perspective.

Chapter 3. The Math

In 3D rendering, all of the spatial relationships between the viewer, light source, object, and planes are represented as vectors. A vector is group of coordinates, in this case, representing three-dimensional space. The following figure illustrates the three principal coordinates: x, y, and z:

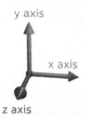

These three axes are orthogonal, that is, mutually perpendicular (forming right angles with each other). The property of orthogonality is very important in the transformations that will be used in rendering. These three axes also conform to the right hand rule or convention, as illustrated in the following figure:

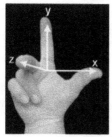

It is most efficient to handle the coordinates as a group or vector. This also simplifies the notation and facilitates calculations, as there are conventions for describing and rules for performing operations on vectors. The first of these is the unit vector. A vector along the x-axis, having length 1, is given the symbol, i. A vector along the y-axis, having length 1, is given the symbol, j. A vector along the z-axis, having length 1, is given the symbol, k. The vector formed by a line starting at the origin (x=0, y=0, z=0) out to some point (x,y,z) can be written $v=xi+yj+zk$. This vector can also be represented by the matrix: [x,y,z].

There are three basic operations with vectors that are foundational to 3D rendering. These are addition, dot (or scalar) product, and cross (or vector) product. The addition of two vectors can be visualized by placing the tail of the second on the head of the first and then drawing a line from the tail of the first to the head of the second, as illustrated below in 2D:

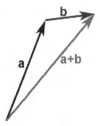

This operation can be represented by the following matrices:

$$\begin{bmatrix} ax \\ ay \\ az \end{bmatrix} + \begin{bmatrix} bx \\ by \\ bz \end{bmatrix} = \begin{bmatrix} ax+bx \\ ay+by \\ az+bz \end{bmatrix}$$

The dot product of two vectors produces a scalar (or single value) and is illustrated in 2D by the following figure:

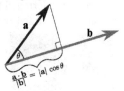

The angle between the two vectors is θ and |a| denotes the length of vector *a*. Another way of looking at the dot product, $a\bullet b=|a|\times|b|\times\cos(\theta)$, is the projection of *a* onto *b*. If *a* were to cast a shadow on *b*, how long would that shadow be? In matrix notation this operation is:

$$\underset{1\times3}{\begin{bmatrix} ax & ay & az \end{bmatrix}} * \underset{3\times1}{\begin{bmatrix} bx \\ by \\ bz \end{bmatrix}} = \underset{1\times1}{\begin{bmatrix} ax*bx+ay*by+az*bz \end{bmatrix}}$$

The following code snippet performs this operation:

```
double DotProduct(double*A,double*B,int n)
  {
  int i;
  double d;
  for(d=i=0;i<n;i++)
  d+=A[i]*B[i];
  return(d);
  }
```

The cross product is where the right hand rule comes in. Where the dot product combines two vectors to produce a scalar, the cross product combines

8

two vectors to produce a third vector. The most basic relationships are presented in terms of the unit vectors, i, j, and k. First, the dot product:

$$i \cdot j = j \cdot k = k \cdot i = 0$$

The above relationships arise from the fact that $\cos(90°)=0$ and the unit vectors form right angles with each other. The cross products are:

$$i \times j = k \ j \times k = i \ k \times i = j$$

The order of these operations, along with the right hand rule, determines the sign of the resultant vector. With a dot product, the order doesn't matter, but with a cross product it does. Reversing the order of the vectors above changes the sign of the resultant:

$$j \times i = -k \ k \times j = -i \ i \times k = -j$$

The cross product can be represented in matrix form by:

$$a \times b = \begin{vmatrix} i & j & k \\ ax & ay & az \\ bx & by & bz \end{vmatrix} = \begin{vmatrix} (ay*bz-az*by)i \\ (az*bx-ax*bz)j \\ (ax*by-ay*bx)k \end{vmatrix}$$

The center expression enclosed in || indicates the determinant. The following code snippet performs this operation:

```
void CrossProduct(double*A,double*B,double*C)
{
C[0]=A[1]*B[2]-A[2]*B[1];
C[1]=A[2]*B[0]-A[0]*B[2];
C[2]=A[0]*B[1]-A[1]*B[0];
}
```

Various transformations can be represented by matrix operations, for instance, scaling. A vector can be made three times as long by the following transformation:

$$\begin{vmatrix} 3 & 0 & 0 \\ 0 & 3 & 0 \\ 0 & 0 & 3 \end{vmatrix} \begin{vmatrix} x \\ y \\ z \end{vmatrix} = \begin{vmatrix} 3x \\ 3y \\ 3z \end{vmatrix}$$

That is, a 3x3 matrix times a 3x1 matrix equals a 3x1 matrix. By convention, the first is the number of rows and the second is the number of columns. When multiplying two matrices, one of size LxM by MxN, the result will be size LxN. The number of columns in the first matrix (M) must equal the number of rows in the second (also M). Matrix multiplication, [A]x[B]=[C], can be expressed by the following formula:

$$C_{l,n} = \sum_{m=1}^{M} A_{i,m} B_{m,n}$$

This is implemented by the following code snippet:

```
void MatrixMultiply(double*A,double*B,double*C, int
    L,int M,int N)
{
int l,m,n;
for(l=0;l<L;l++)
for(n=0;n<N;n++)
 for(C[N*l+n]=m=0;m<M;m++)
 C[N*l+n]+=A[M*l+m]*B[N*m+n];
}
```

A more general scaling, x*Sx, y*Sy, z*Sz, would be performed by the following matrix operation:

$$
\begin{vmatrix} Sx & 0 & 0 \\ 0 & Sy & 0 \\ 0 & 0 & Sz \end{vmatrix} * \begin{vmatrix} x \\ y \\ z \end{vmatrix} = \begin{vmatrix} x*Sx \\ y*Sy \\ z*Sz \end{vmatrix}
$$

Some transformations require adding a constant to the resultant (or right hand side) of the operation. This is accomplished by adding a fourth component or augmenting the vector and matrix, as in:

$$
\begin{vmatrix} Sx & 0 & 0 & 0 \\ 0 & Sy & 0 & 0 \\ 0 & 0 & Sz & 0 \\ 0 & 0 & 0 & C \end{vmatrix} * \begin{vmatrix} x \\ y \\ z \\ 1 \end{vmatrix} = \begin{vmatrix} x*Sx \\ y*Sy \\ z*Sz \\ C \end{vmatrix}
$$

Rotations are performed about one axis at a time. A rotation about the x-axis by an angle θ is performed by the following matrix operation:

$$
\begin{vmatrix} 1 & 0 & 0 \\ 0 & \cos(\theta) & -\sin(\theta) \\ 0 & \sin(\theta) & \cos(\theta) \end{vmatrix}
$$

A rotation about the y-axis by an angle φ is performed by the following matrix operation:

$$
\begin{vmatrix} \cos(\phi) & 0 & \sin(\phi) \\ 0 & 1 & 0 \\ -\sin(\phi) & 0 & \cos(\phi) \end{vmatrix}
$$

A rotation about the z-axis by an angle ψ is performed by the following matrix operation:

$$\begin{bmatrix} \cos(\psi) & -\sin(\psi) & 0 \\ \sin(\psi) & \cos(\psi) & 0 \\ 0 & 0 & 1 \end{bmatrix}$$

These operations are performed by the following code snippet:

```
void RotateX(double*V,double*U,double theta)
{
double R[3*3];
R[0]=1.;R[1]=0.  ;R[2]=0.;
R[3]=0.;R[4]=cos(theta);R[5]=-sin(theta);
R[6]=0.;R[7]=sin(theta);R[8]= cos(theta);
MatrixMultiply(R,V,U,3,3,1);
}
void RotateY(double*V,double*U,double phi)
{
double R[3*3];
R[0]= cos(phi);R[1]=0.;R[2]=sin(phi);
R[3]=0.  ;R[4]=1.;R[5]=0.;
R[6]=-sin(phi);R[7]=0.;R[8]=cos(phi);
MatrixMultiply(R,V,U,3,3,1);
}
void RotateZ(double*V,double*U,double psi)
{
double R[3*3];
R[0]=cos(psi);R[1]=-sin(psi);R[2]=0.;
R[3]=sin(psi);R[4]= cos(psi);R[5]=0.;
R[6]=0.  ;R[7]=0.  ;R[8]=1.;
MatrixMultiply(R,V,U,3,3,1);
}
```

OpenGL® performs these operations for you, but it is important to understand what it's doing so that you can direct the library to do what intend. More transformations and vector operations will be presented in Chapter 14, rendering without OpenGL®.

11

Chapter 4. The Objects

By computational necessity, the geometric representation of a 3D scene is composed of individual objects. Each of these objects must be broken down into polygons, as illustrated below:

The most basic polygon would be a line, but reflecting light requires a surface. The simplest polygon that defines a surface is a triangle. The surface of the teapot above has been described by an assemblage of triangles. Pairs of triangles in some regions could be combined, as illustrated below:

There is no spatial ambiguity in a polygon having only three distinct vertices, as the three points define a unique plane. There is, however, spatial ambiguity in any polygon having more than three vertices, as illustrated below:

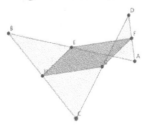

as any combination of three may define a different plane. There is also an orientation that is associated with polygons, as it is important to know whether you are looking at the front or the back side of something. The convention for polygon orientation follows from the right hand rule for vectors. This orientation is illustrated in the following figure:

13

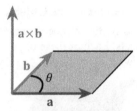

The cross product of the two vectors, *a* and *b*, lying in the plane forms the outward normal area vector *a×b*. Each polygon on the surface has an associated outward normal vector, as illustrated in this next figure:

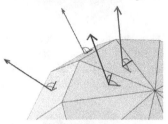

Outward normal area vectors for sphere look like this:

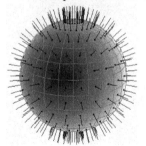

The cross product of the vectors lying in the plane form the outward normal, which determines the relationship between that part of the surface and the light source.

Chapter 5. The Lighting

There are different types of light sources, including point and spot lights:

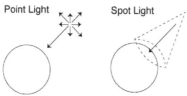

Light is also classified as being either directional or ambient: as if coming from a particular source or as if coming from everywhere:

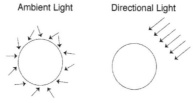

The light source may be white (containing all colors) or contain only some colors. The position of the light source relative to the objects and viewer is also important. Defining the light source (or sources) is one of the first steps in rendering the 3D scene.

Of the examples contained in the online archive, the OpenGL® Move Light and Mesa Teapot examples are the best illustrations of light source positioning.

Chapter 6. Shading, Scattering, and Texture

One of the most important aspects of 3D rendering is modeling how the surface of the objects reacts to lighting. The simplest model of light is illustrated in the following figure:

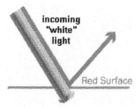

This next figure illustrates what this looks like for a familiar object:

The interaction between real light and actual surfaces is more complex than this, as illustrated below:

A shiny surface will produce a specular reflection and a rough surface will produce a diffuse reflection. A surface may even change the color of the light, as illustrated in this next figure:

The more realistic you want objects to appear, the more effort you will have to put into the light/surface interactions. The OpenGL® library can handle several levels of complexity, but it does have limitations that will be discussed later. The various options in lighting and surfaces provided by OpenGL® are illustrated in the teapots example that is included in the SDK:

17

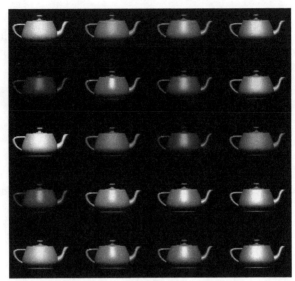

Some of the combinations above look like plastic, while others look metallic or ceramic. The polygons defining the teapot are the same in each case.

Chapter 7. Shadows, Reflections, and Stenciling

Shadows, reflections, and other similar scene enhancements are implemented using stenciling and multiple drawing passes. Dino shade is a good example of this. Consider the following explanation by the developer, Mark J. Kilgard:

> We can eliminate the visual "artifact" of seeing the "flipped" dinosaur underneath the floor by using stencil. The idea is to draw the floor without color or depth. Update but so that a stencil value of one is where the floor will be. Later when rendering the dinosaur reflection, only update pixels with a stencil value of 1 to make sure the reflection is only on the floor, not below the floor.

> Back face culling will be used to only draw either the top or the bottom floor. This produces a floor with two distinct appearances. The top floor surface is dark red and reflective. The bottom floor surface is dark blue and not reflective.

> Draw the floor with stencil value 3. This assures that the shadow will only be drawn once per floor pixel (and only on the floor pixels).

> Only render where stencil is set above 2 (i.e., 3 where the top floor is). Update stencil with 2 where the shadow gets drawn so we don't redraw the shadow.

The following section of code from this example that illustrates how this is implemented:

```
if((stencilReflection&&renderReflection)||
   (stencilShadow&&renderShadow))
   glClear(GL_COLOR_BUFFER_BIT|GL_DEPTH_BUFFER_BIT|
   GL_STENCIL_BUFFER_BIT);
else
   glClear(GL_COLOR_BUFFER_BIT|GL_DEPTH_BUFFER_BIT);
glDisable(GL_DEPTH_TEST);
glColorMask(GL_FALSE,GL_FALSE,GL_FALSE,GL_FALSE);
glEnable(GL_STENCIL_TEST);
glStencilOp(GL_REPLACE,GL_REPLACE,GL_REPLACE);
glStencilFunc(GL_ALWAYS,1,0xFFFFFFFF);
drawFloor();
glColorMask(GL_TRUE,GL_TRUE,GL_TRUE,GL_TRUE);
glEnable(GL_DEPTH_TEST);
glStencilFunc(GL_EQUAL,1,0xFFFFFFFF);
glStencilOp(GL_KEEP,GL_KEEP,GL_KEEP);
```

The examples that use stenciling to produce visual effects include: Chess, Dino Draw, Dino Shade, Reflect Dino, Reflect 2, and Shapes. The Knight's Tour, Stonehenge 2, and View3DS examples use stenciling to identify objects but not for visual effects.[3]

The reflect example appears to be a reflection, but is actually a clever painting and does not use stenciling. Instead, this example uses mipmaps to

---

[3] See Appendix G for details.

define the relationship between the flat image of a tree and the curved surface of the torus, as in the following code snippet:

```
gluBuild2DMipmaps(GL_TEXTURE_2D,format,w,h,GL_RGB,
    GL_UNSIGNED_BYTE,image);
glTexParameterfv(GL_TEXTURE_2D,GL_TEXTURE_WRAP_S,
    GL_REPEAT);
glTexParameterfv(GL_TEXTURE_2D,GL_TEXTURE_WRAP_T,
    GL_REPEAT);
glTexEnvfv(GL_TEXTURE_ENV,GL_TEXTURE_ENV_MODE,
    GL_MODULATE);
cube=glGenLists(1);
BuildCube();
cage=glGenLists(2);
BuildCage();
cylinder=glGenLists(3);
BuildCylinder(60);
torus=glGenLists(4);
BuildTorus(0.65,20,.85,65);
genericObject=torus;
```

The maps and textures are prepared before allocating the rendering lists and building the objects. This is more elaborate in appearance than the Earth & Moon example, but the method is the same.

Chapter 8. Rendering

Methods for rendering 3D objects can be divided into two categories: 1) ray tracing and 2) everything else. Ray tracing is like particle tracking for photons, only more computationally intensive. Ray tracing produces the most realistic results, but is entirely impractical for anything that is interactive. Ray tracing requires a server farm and a budget the size of most countries' GDP. OpenGL® doesn't use ray tracing and we're not going to cover it in this book.

The two most common rendering methods that don't involve ray tracing are: 1) hidden surface and 2) Z-buffering. The hidden surface method is also much too computationally intensive to be practical in this context. The Z-buffering method of rendering is called by several names, including rasterization and shading, but these are misnomers. The Z-buffering method is by far the fastest method and can produce acceptable results with reasonable effort.

The concept of Z-buffering is quite simple: Draw the projection of each element of each object one pixel at a time. If you carry along all of the terms, each pixel will have a depth associated with it (i.e., a distance from the viewer). If the latest pixel is closer to the observer than the one previous one, replace it; otherwise discard it.

Z-buffering requires a depth plane as well as a color plane. OpenGL® most often uses a single-precision (32-bit) floating-point Z-buffer, although there are several other options. All of the OpenGL® calls that pass floating-point values use single-precision (32-bit) types. This choice of Z-buffer depth achieves good quality and speed.[4]

---

[4] For more options see Appendix C.

Chapter 9. Painting

Whether you're using OpenGL® or some other library, the scene is rendered in memory and then painted onto the display after it is complete. With OpenGL® the painting step is performed by calling SwapBuffers(). Call glutSwapBuffers() when using the OpenGL® GLUT® library.

The long ago 2 and spin cube examples use BitBlt() to paint the image from memory onto the display. The long ago 1, Stonehenge 3, and View3D examples use InvalidateRect() or RedrawWindow() to force the graphics window to repaint (i.e., receive the WM_PAINT message) and then SetDIBitsToDevice() to paint the bitmap from memory onto the display. The difference between these last two groups is necessitated by the pixel depth. The long ago 2 and spin cube images can be created in the same depth as the display using WinAPI function calls and bitmap handles; whereas, the long ago 1, Stonehenge 3, and View3D images are always 8 bits/pixel–regardless of the display color depth–and are created by direct manipulation of each pixel (i.e., each byte in the bitmap).

Chapter 10. 3D Rendering with OpenGL

There are many books and articles on rendering 3D objects using OpenGL®. This book is a supplement to, not a replacement for, such texts. There are at least two reasons for this book. First, OpenGL® was developed on and for the Unix® O/S. Most of the available examples assume you will be building and running these on either Unix® or Linux®.

Microsoft® supported OpenGL® before it established their proprietary product, DirectX®, but has since dismissed OpenGL® and made various changes to the Visual Studio® C compiler so that it will no longer compile the original examples. Second, there are essential aspects of working with OpenGL® that are not well explained within the context of the Windows® O/S. There are also essential aspects of 3D rendering that are assumed to be common knowledge in the OpenGL® literature that are truly arcane outside of Unix®.

For example, OpenGL® texture files are problematic in Windows®. The RGB, BW, and TEX file formats are unknown outside of Unix®. Granted, the BMP file format is unique to Windows® and not recognized on the WWW, but the GIF, PNG, JPG, and TIF file formats are universally recognized. It requires a special image editing tool, endless format conversions, or rewriting the texture code in order to work with these non-Unix formats. I have done the latter for you.

Some C compilers will recognize a forward or backslash as a path separator, but others will not. The OpenGL® examples do not follow other conventions, for instance, the use of <header.h> to indicate a file located in a common folder vs. "header.h" to indicate a local file in the current folder. These and other differences result in an explosion of compiler errors that can be daunting.

The OpenGL® examples assume both a console and a graphic application window. The examples originally came with the following main program statement:

```
int main(int argc,char**argv,char**envp)
```

This is the standard main program for a console application.[5] While this does work with recent versions, the expected main program statement for a Windows® program is the following:

```
int WINAPI WinMain(HINSTANCE hInstance,HINSTANCE
    hPrev,char*lpszLine,int nShow)
```

In this case, the parsed command line is available, but not as an argument:

```
extern int __argc;
extern char**__argv;
extern char**_environ;
```

---

[5] Users familiar with Windows® and unfamiliar with Unix® or Linux® mistakenly refer to a console application as a DOS box. The more accurate Windows® term for such is a command prompt.

Some of the OpenGL® examples include keyboard input, but it is handled entirely different from the standard for Windows® programs. Getting OpenGL® to work seamlessly within the context of Windows® is not burdensome or overly complicated, but it isn't well documented. That is the object of this book.

All of the modified examples accompanying this book will compile with the latest version of Visual Studio® and are available on the web free of charge. They are all contained in a single ZIP file, separated into individual folders. This archive includes an Excel® spreadsheet that lists each example and can be sorted by category.

The essential parts of the Visual Studio® C compiler are available free of charge on the Microsoft® web site. Download the W7.1 SDK and the W7 DDK. After you install these, combine all of the bin, lib, and include folders for the x86 platform into a single location: C:\VC32. That and these examples are all you need to get started.

Getting Started

I recommend that you start with the simplest examples, for instance, ACCNOT or SCENE, which have simple lighting and basic shapes. Use GLUT, the OpenGL® Utility Toolkit, and GLAUX, the OpenGL® Auxiliary Library, to do most of the work for you. Familiarize yourself with the lighting and point-of-view. When you are comfortable with one, move on to another example and then up to a higher level, for instance PLANETUP, which has a large and small wireframe sphere (Earth & Moon) that you can rotate and orbit by pressing the arrow keys.

Chapter 11. The OpenGL® Examples

The over fifty examples contained in the online archive (see Appendix A) cover most aspects of 3D rendering. They also vary considerably in complexity. I suggest starting with the simplest examples and working your way up to the more complex.

The Simplest Examples

The simplest examples are accnot, Planet Up, scclrlt, scene, Tea Amb, and T-Prim. I suggest you start with accnot to get the basics of shape generation. Then move on to scene and scclrlt to get the basics of lighting. Accnot is shown below:

Animated Examples

Animation is one of the main reasons for 3D rendering. The elements of animation included in these examples can be separated into three categories: 1) rotations and translations, 2) objects that change in shape, 3) user-controlled motions. The examples that fall into this first category include: Atlantis, Blender, Bounce, Chess, Cube Map, Dino Ball, Dino Draw, Dino Shade, Dino Spin, Earth & Moon, Gears, Gear Train, Ideas, Lorenz, Occlude, Olympic Rings, Planet Up, Point Burst, Puzzle, Reflect, Reflect Dino, Reflect 2, and Roller Coaster. The examples that fall into the second category include: Blue Pony, Morph3D, and Origami. The examples that fall into the third category include: Knight's Tour, Move Light, Shapes, Sky Fly, Stonehenge 1, Stonehenge 2, Stonehenge 3, T-Select, View3D, and View3DS.

I suggest you start with Planet Up, then Bounce, then Olympic Rings and Atlantis. After you have mastered these, move on to Morph3D and Blue Pony. When you have mastered these, move on to Origami. The Ideas and Sky Fly examples are quite complex. The dinosaur examples are between these last two groups in complexity. I would recommend them next.

Dinosaurs

Five of the examples from the OpenGL® Software Development Kit that involve drawing a simple dinosaur have been included in the online archive. These illustrate many important concepts and steps in the development of a complete three-dimensional rendering system. These are listed below in order of

27

increasing complexity: 1) Dino Ball, 2) Dino Draw, 3) Dino Spin, 4) Reflect Dino, and 5) Dino Shade.

The first three illustrate creating and drawing the dinosaur object. The fourth illustrates creating a reflection. The fifth illustrates shadow, reflection, and a moving light source. The combined result is shown below:

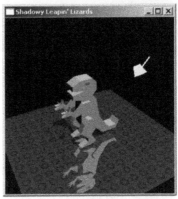

The variable rate of bounce in the dinosaur examples is realistic. Bouncing is a case of sinusoidal motion. These illustrate more complex motion than simple rotation. I suggest that you go through each of these examples, changing a few things (colors, lighting, size), and recompile.

Blue Pony

Brian Paul's Blue Pony example is a classic. It's simple, compact, entertaining, and illustrates several important concepts. The entire source code is less than 500 lines long and includes painting the OpenGL® logo on a billboard, creating the pony, articulating the legs, and prancing it around.

The structure of this program is simple and straightforward. The section of code that paints the logo is less than 20 lines long. It would be a good exercise to add grass to the ground and then a realistic coat of hair to the pony. Refer to the Earth & Moon example on how to add these two textures as resources in a RC file. The extra step to compile the resource file is in _compile.bat in the Earth &

Moon folder. Remember that the height and width of the textures must be a power of 2.

<u>Earth & Moon</u>

This example is the simplest example of shape rendering (a single call to draw a sphere), the simplest animation (rotation), and the simplest draping a texture over a surface. The size of the Moon relative to the Earth is correct, but the distance between them is greatly reduced. The rotation is in the correct direction, but the Moon orbital period is much shorter than actual.

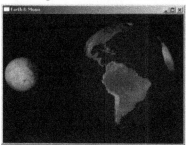

This example uses gluSphere(), which is in the GLUT library. This library contains similar functions to create a cone, cylinder, disk, and partial disk. These are defined in glu.h. Use of these functions facilitates draping the texture over the shape through the use of quadrics. A quadric is a second order surface. I suggest you try this same thing with the other shapes and other textures. Remember that the height and width of the textures must be a power of 2.

The GLAUX library has more functions to create a variety of geometric objects, including:

auxSolidBox()	auxWireBox()
auxSolidCone()	auxWireCone()
auxSolidCube()	auxWireCube()
auxSolidCylinder()	auxWireCylinder()
auxSolidDodecahedron()	auxWireDodecahedron()
auxSolidIcosahedron()	auxWireIcosahedron()
auxSolidOctahedron()	auxWireOctahedron()
auxSolidSphere()	auxWireSphere()
auxSolidTeapot()	auxWireTeapot()
auxSolidTetrahedron()	auxWireTetrahedron()
auxSolidTorus()	auxWireTorus()

If you use the aux function calls you will need to use glBindTexture() and glTexCoord2d() or one of its variants to map the textures onto the objectss. The examples that include calls to auxSolid() include: accnot, alpha3d, dofnot, Fog, Material, Move Light, scclrlt, Scene, Tea Amb, Teapots, TexGen. The examples

29

that include calls to glTexCoor() include: Blue Pony, Chess, Cube Map, Dino Shade, Knight's Tour, Perf Draw, Point Burst, Reflect 2, Teapot, View3DS. I suggest you first try replacing the call to gluSphere() with auxSolidSphere() and then add the calls to glTexCoord().

Surfaces & Lighting Examples

In addition to the dinosaurs, there are ten examples that primarily illustrate surfaces and lighting. These are: alpha3d, dof not, fog, ideas, material, reflect, scclrlt, scene, teapot, and teapots. As you have already mastered scclrlt and scene, I suggest starting with teapots and material. Teapot is quite complex and I suggest you not work with this until after you have mastered most of the other examples. The teapots were shown in the chapter on shading, scattering, & reflecting. The material example is shown below:

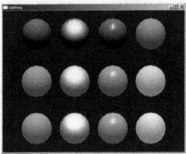

Examples of Surface Material Effects

Images draped over an object are called textures. OpenGL® requires that textures be 24-bit (red-green-blue). Textures must also have a width and height that are a power of 2. Several of the examples use files with extension RGB or BW. These are not recognized by any Windows® program, but you can read them and convert them to BMP using the code in readtex.c, which can be found in the Blue Pony, Iso-Surf, Reflect, Reflect 2, and Teapot folders.

You will find code to read and write BMP, GIF, and JPG files in the spin cube folder. You will also find code that uses Windows® API calls to change the bits/pixel and dimensions of an image in the View3DS folder. You can read the textures after the application begins, as in the Reflect and Teapot examples, or load them as resources, as in the Blue Pony and Earth & Moon examples.

You can use quadrics and the GLUT library or calls to glTexCoord() to associate the textures with the locations on the surface of your objects. I suggest starting with the former and moving to the latter. I recommend Earth & Moon, Knight's Tour, Reflect, and Stonehenge 2 as examples of more complex texture mappings. You should also find the View3DS example quite helpful.

Chapter 12. Stonehenge 1-2-3

There are three examples included in the online archive representing Stonehenge: 1) the original one that came with the OpenGL® Software Development Kit, 2) one that is a little more complicated and has three-dimensional controls, and 3) this one that doesn't use OpenGL®. This last example contains all the code necessary to render 3D objects, including the primitive calculations. These three examples illustrate many different things.

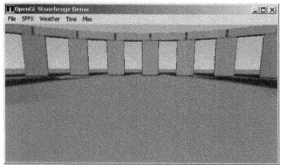

The first example illustrates several basic effects, including: lighting, shadows, fog, telescope view, and anti-aliasing. It also illustrates simulated weather conditions, including: clear, foggy, very foggy, and rainy. The orientation and position of the light source is supposed to account for the position of the sun, but doesn't work very well. The OpenGL® Move Light and Mesa Teapot examples are much better examples of light source positioning. The OpenGL® Dino Shade example is also helpful. The Stonehenge demo mode shows how to build complex animations.

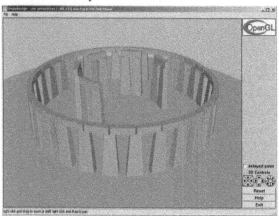

The second example is a more complete Windows® program, with buttons and greater control over where the rendering is painted. It has custom controls for three-dimensional rotation and translation and accepts input from the keyboard, including the arrow keys, coupled with the alt and control keys.

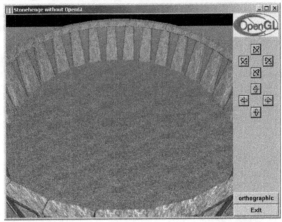

The third example is also a complete Windows® program with a different set of custom buttons to control rotation and view. This example does not use OpenGL®, rather it includes all of the primitive rendering calculations necessary, including draping of textures (or bitmaps) over objects.

Chapter 13. The 3D Studio® Model Viewer

This example illustrates many features of 3D rendering with OpenGL® as well as Windows® applications. It includes: menus, keyboard input, custom controls, reading textures, reading a binary file, selecting a pixel format, painting in a child window, constructing complex objects from geometric primitives, lighting, perspective, and texture mapping.

This program loads and displays a 3D Studio® model. Three models are included (T-Rex, elephant, and sheep). Countless models are available free online. One good source is TurboSquid:

https://www.turbosquid.com/Search/3D-Models/free

The T-Rex model is shown here:

These models often come as a ZIP file with the textures embedded. A good exercise would be to add the code to open the zip file and read the model and textures. I have provided code elsewhere to read and write ZIP files from the disk or from memory. The latter allows you to include a ZIP file as a binary resource inside a Windows® application.

This example is a good illustration of how to create and display complex models that are defined by a mesh and one or more textures. The basic structures are elements and nodes. These are defined as:

```
typedef struct{int i,j,k,m;DWORD color;}ELEM;
typedef struct{float u,v,x,y,z;}NODE;
```

Each element has three or more nodes, whose indices are identified by i, j, and k. Each element also has a color and possibly a material (or texture (or bitmap)) identified by m. Each node has a coordinate in three-dimensional space defined by x, y, and z. The additional variables u and v identify the corresponding location within the material (or texture) m. The lower left corner of the texture is (0,0) and the upper right corner is (1,1). These coordinates are regardless of the width and height of the texture in pixels. As OpenGL® uses single precision floats, there is no point defining these as double precision. The following code snippet illustrates how to render such a mesh.

```
for(l=0;l<elems;l++)
{
i=elem[l].i;
j=elem[l].j;
k=elem[l].k;
m=elem[l].m;
v1[0]=(node[i].x-xc)/s;
v1[1]=(node[i].y-yc)/s;
v1[2]=(node[i].z-zc)/s;
v2[0]=(node[j].x-xc)/s;
v2[1]=(node[j].y-yc)/s;
v2[2]=(node[j].z-zc)/s;
v3[0]=(node[k].x-xc)/s;
v3[1]=(node[k].y-yc)/s;
v3[2]=(node[k].z-zc)/s;
p[0]=v2[0]-v1[0];
p[1]=v2[1]-v1[1];
p[2]=v2[2]-v1[2];
q[0]=v3[0]-v1[0];
q[1]=v3[1]-v1[1];
q[2]=v3[2]-v1[2];
CrossProduct(p,q,n);
if(textures&&fill_polygons&&m>=0)
 {
 glColor(WHITE);
 glEnable(GL_TEXTURE_2D);
 glBindTexture(GL_TEXTURE_2D,texture[m]);
 glBegin(GL_TRIANGLES);
 glNormal3fv(n);
 glTexCoord2d(node[i].u,node[i].v);
 glVertex3fv(v1);
 glTexCoord2d(node[j].u,node[j].v);
 glVertex3fv(v2);
 glTexCoord2d(node[k].u,node[k].v);
 glVertex3fv(v3);
 glEnd();
 }
else
 {
 glDisable(GL_TEXTURE_2D);
 glColor(elem.color);
 glBegin(GL_TRIANGLES);
 glNormal3fv(n);
 glVertex3fv(v1);
 glVertex3fv(v2);
 glVertex3fv(v3);
 glEnd();
 }
```

The material can change from one element to the other, so this is inside the loop. It doesn't take long to enable or disable textures or to bind a particular texture. In this case, binding is simply setting an index. The more computationally intensive task has already been done and stored in the coordinates u and v.

In order to properly manage the relationship between lighting and surfaces—whether or not they have a texture—you must define the outward normal of each element. This is accomplished above by creating two vectors: one from nodes i to j and another from i to k. The cross product of these two vectors is the outward normal.

You must scale and center the objects. This is accomplished above by subtracting the coordinates from the centroid (xc, yc, zc) and dividing by the scaling factor, s. The value of s depends on the scaling of the model as well as the view setup.

Chapter 14. 3D Rendering without OpenGL

There are two reasons I can think of that you might want to render 3D objects without this powerful system: 1) OpenGL® it isn't compatible with your system and 2) you don't want to be locked into 24-bit color depth. Perhaps the most compelling reason for not wanting to be locked into 24-bit color depth is to produce animated GIFs.

Since the dawn of the World Wide Web, the standard for animations has been the GIF–not the ASF, AVI, MOV, MPG, SWF, or WMV. GIFs are limited to 256 colors. The JPG and similar formats based on lossy compression are fine for pictures, but not for graphs, line drawings, or anything else that has clear boundaries. Creating an animation in 24 bits/pixel color and then reducing it to 8 bits/pixel produces undesirable results in both quality and compression.

Rather than using 24 bits/pixel color, it is possible to produce quality renderings using only 42 colors: black, white, blue, brown, cyan, green, magenta, orange, purple, red, yellow, and 31 shades of gray. As this is less than 64, the resulting images require only 6 bits and can be adequately compressed without loss of information. Gradations of shade are created by dithering the primary color with the range of black to gray to white.

This same shading scheme was used by Tecplot® through Version 8. Tecplot® switched to OpenGL® and 24-bit colors with Version 9. The earlier versions of Tecplot® produced animations using the Raster Meta File format (RM), which could be easily converted to GIF[6]. More recent versions of Tecplot® produce Audio Visual Interleave (AVI) files, which don't compress nearly as well and add nothing in the way of quality.

To end up with a clean, compact animation using only
8 bits/pixel you must render it with this goal in mind.

The scene is stored in a bitmap plus a depth buffer. A stencil buffer is optional. Unless you implement special mixed floating-point and integer calculations, as is the case with OpenGL®, you might as well use double-precision floating-point numbers for the depth buffer. I use 8-bit color so that there is one byte per pixel in the bitmap. This also simplifies addressing. Windows® requires the width of the bitmap to be a multiple of 4.

The basic steps in rendering are: 1) clear the bitmap and Z-buffer, 2) render the objects, and 3) paint the bitmap onto the display. To clear the bitmap, set all values to the background color with memset(). To clear the Z-buffer, set all the values to DBL_MAX (i.e., infinitely far from the observer).

All objects must be broken down into lines or triangles and rendered one at a time. These 2 or 3 points are transformed using the rotations, translations, and scalings defined in Chapter 3. Three distinct points (i.e., a triangle) define a

---

[6] A free RM to GIF conversion tool with source code is available on my web site.

plane in three-dimensional space. This plane can be described mathematically by a*x+b*y+c*z=1, where a, b, and c are constants. In the case of a line, either a or b is zero. Replace every pixel along the line (or within the triangle) if the value of z is less than the previous value, in which case, replacing the value of z as well.

The index of the color (or shade of gray) that goes into the bitmap depends on the color of the surface (or the color of the texture mapped onto the surface) and the angle of the surface with respect to the light source(s). If the sum of x+y is odd, an appropriate shade of gray is selected. If the sum of x+y is even, the base color is selected.

Different algorithms for light and surface interaction can be used to produce various effects. The simplest would be either 0 (black) or 1 (white), depending on whether the surface is toward or away from the light source(s). The next level of complexity would be $\rho=(1-\cos(\varsigma))/2$, where ς is the angle between the outward normal of the surface and the light source. When $\varsigma=0°$, $\rho=0$ (black) and when $\varsigma=180°$, $\rho=1$ (white).

The outward normal is calculated using the cross product as described in Chapter 3. Don't paint the back side of surfaces, as these point away from the observer. The back side of objects can be identified by the angle between the outward normal and the viewer (i.e., $\varsigma<90°$ pointing away from the viewer and $\varsigma>90°$ pointing toward the viewer).

The following structures facilitate these operations:

```
typedef struct tagCOLOR{
    BYTE b;
    BYTE g;
    BYTE r;
    }COLOR;
typedef struct tagVECTOR{
    double x;
    double y;
    double z;
    double w;
    }VECTOR;
typedef struct tagVERTEX{
    COLOR c;
    VECTOR p;
    VECTOR n;
    }VERTEX;
typedef struct tagMATRIX{
    VECTOR x;
    VECTOR y;
    VECTOR z;
    VECTOR w;
    }MATRIX;
```

```
MATRIX Identity={{1,0,0,0},{0,1,0,0},
   {0,0,1,0},{0,0,0,1}};
```
The following functions perform the necessary matrix operations:
```
VECTOR Vector(double x,double y,double z,double w)
{
static VECTOR P;
P.x=x;
P.y=y;
P.z=z;
P.w=w;
return(P);
}
MATRIX Matrix(VECTOR Vx,VECTOR Vy,VECTOR Vz,VECTOR Vw)
{
static MATRIX M;
M.x=Vx;
M.y=Vy;
M.z=Vz;
M.w=Vw;
return(M);
}
VERTEX Vertex(VECTOR p,COLOR c)
{
static VERTEX V;
V.c=c;
V.p=p;
return(V);
}
double Euclidean(VECTOR P)
{
return(sqrt(P.x*P.x+P.y*P.y+P.z*P.z+P.w*P.w));
}
double DotProduct(VECTOR P,VECTOR Q)
{
return(P.x*Q.x+P.y*Q.y+P.z*Q.z+P.w*Q.w);
}
VECTOR CrossProduct(VECTOR P,VECTOR Q)
{
static VECTOR R;
R.x=P.y*Q.z-P.z*Q.y;
R.y=P.z*Q.x-P.x*Q.z;
R.z=P.x*Q.y-P.y*Q.x;
R.w=P.w*Q.w;
return(R);
}
VECTOR Direction(VECTOR P,VECTOR Q)
{
static VECTOR R;
R.x=Q.x-P.x;
```

39

```
R.y=Q.y-P.y;
R.z=Q.z-P.z;
R.w=Q.w-P.w;
return(R);
}
VECTOR Normalize(VECTOR P)
{
static VECTOR N;
double d=Euclidean(P);
if(d>0.)
  {
  N.x=P.x/d;
  N.y=P.y/d;
  N.z=P.z/d;
  N.w=P.w/d;
  }
else
  {
  N.x=P.x;
  N.y=P.y;
  N.z=P.z;
  N.w=P.w;
  }
return(N);
}
void MatrixMultiply(double*A,double*B,double*C,int l,
    int n,int m)
{
int i,j,k;
for(i=0;i<l;i++)
  for(j=0;j<m;j++)
    for(C[m*i+j]=k=0;k<n;k++)
      C[m*i+j]+=A[n*i+k]*B[m*k+j];
}
```

The following functions perform rotations, translations, and scaling of points:

```
void TranslateObjective(double x,double y,double z)
{
MATRIX Q=Transform[matrix_stack];
MATRIX P=Identity;
P.x.w=x;
P.y.w=y;
P.z.w=z;
MatrixMultiply((double*)&Q,(double*)&P,
  (double*)(Transform+matrix_stack),4,4,4);
}
void ScaleObjective(double x,double y,double z)
{
```

```
MATRIX Q=Transform[matrix_stack];
MATRIX P=Identity;
P.x.x=x;
P.y.y=y;
P.z.z=z;
MatrixMultiply((double*)&Q,(double*)&P,
  (double*)(Transform+matrix_stack),4,4,4);
}
void RotateObjective(double a,double b,double c)
{
MATRIX P,Q;
Q=Transform[matrix_stack];
P=Identity;
P.y.y=cos(a);P.y.z=-sin(a);
P.z.y=sin(a);P.z.z= cos(a);
MatrixMultiply((double*)&Q,(double*)&P,
  (double*)(Transform+matrix_stack),4,4,4);
Q=Transform[matrix_stack];
P=Identity;
P.x.x=cos(b);P.x.z=-sin(b);
P.z.x=sin(b);P.z.z= cos(b);
MatrixMultiply((double*)&Q,(double*)&P,
  (double*)(Transform+matrix_stack),4,4,4);
Q=Transform[matrix_stack];
P=Identity;
P.x.x=cos(c);P.x.y=-sin(c);
P.y.x=sin(c);P.y.y= cos(c);
MatrixMultiply((double*)&Q,(double*)&P,
  (double*)(Transform+matrix_stack),4,4,4);
}
```

The following functions manipulate a stack of transforms that can be stored and retrieved in the same way as glPushMatrix() and glPopMatrix():

```
MATRIX Transform[8];
int matrix_stack;
void PushTransform()
{
if(++matrix_stack>=sizeof(Transform)/sizeof(MATRIX))
  Abort(__LINE__,"objective matrix stack overflow");
Transform[matrix_stack]=Transform[matrix_stack-1];
}
void PopTransform()
{
if(--matrix_stack<0)
  Abort(__LINE__,"objective matrix stack underflow");
}
```

The following functions render a line and triangle, respectively:

```
void RenderLine(int x1,int y1,int x2,int y2,BYTE c)
{
```

```
int dx,dy,x,y;
if(abs(x2-x1)>abs(y2-y1))
  {
  if(x1>x2)
    {
    x=x2;
    x2=x1;
    x1=x;
    y=y2;
    y2=y1;
    y1=y;
    }
  dx=x2-x1;
  dy=y2-y1;
  if(dx!=0)
    {
    for(x=x1;x<=x2;x++)
      {
      if(x<0)
        continue;
      if(x>=Scene.w)
        break;
      y=y1+dy*(x-x1)/dx;
      if(y<0)
        continue;
      if(y>=Scene.h)
        continue;
      Scene.c[Scene.w*y+x]=c;
      }
    }
  else
    {
    if(y1>=0&&y1<Scene.h)
      {
      for(x=x1;x<=x2;x++)
        {
        if(x<0)
          continue;
        if(x>=Scene.w)
          break;
        Scene.c[Scene.w*y1+x]=c;
        }
      }
    }
  }
else
  {
  if(y1>y2)
    {
```

```
        y=y2;
        y2=y1;
        y1=y;
        x=x2;
        x2=x1;
        x1=x;
        }
    dx=x2-x1;
    dy=y2-y1;
    if(dy!=0)
        {
        for(y=y1;y<=y2;y++)
          {
          if(y<0)
            continue;
          if(y>=Scene.h)
            break;
          x=x1+dx*(y-y1)/dy;
          if(x<0)
            continue;
          if(x>=Scene.w)
            continue;
          Scene.c[Scene.w*y+x]=c;
          }
        }
    else
        {
        if(x1>=0&&x1<Scene.w)
          {
          for(y=y1;y<=y2;y++)
            {
            if(y<0)
              continue;
            if(y>=Scene.h)
              break;
            Scene.c[Scene.w*y+x1]=c;
            }
          }
        }
    }
}

void OutlineTriangle(NODE*n1,NODE*n2,NODE*n3,BYTE c)
  {
  int x1,x2,x3,y1,y2,y3;
  x1=nint(n1->x);
  y1=nint(n1->y);
  x2=nint(n2->x);
  y2=nint(n2->y);
```

43

```
  x3=nint(n3->x);
  y3=nint(n3->y);
  RenderLine(x1,y1,x2,y2,c);
  RenderLine(x2,y2,x3,y3,c);
  RenderLine(x3,y3,x1,y1,c);
  }

void RenderTriangle(NODE*n1,NODE*n2,NODE*n3,BYTE c)
  {
  int i,x,x1,x2,x3,xa,xb,y,y1,y2,y3,ya,yb;
  double
    Det,D11,D12,D13,D21,D22,D23,D31,D32,D33,Z,Zo,Zx,Zy;
  BYTE g,s;
  NODE w1,w2,w3;

/* determine equation of projected plane of element */

  Det=(n2->x-n1->x)*(n3->y-n2->y)-(n3->x-n2->x)*(n2->y-
  n1->y);
  if(fabs(Det)>10.)
    {
    D11=(n2->x*n3->y-n3->x*n2->y)/Det;
    D12=(n3->x*n1->y-n1->x*n3->y)/Det;
    D13=(n1->x*n2->y-n2->x*n1->y)/Det;
    D21=(n2->y-n3->y)/Det;
    D22=(n3->y-n1->y)/Det;
    D23=(n1->y-n2->y)/Det;
    D31=(n3->x-n2->x)/Det;
    D32=(n1->x-n3->x)/Det;
    D33=(n2->x-n1->x)/Det;
    Zo=n1->z*D11+n2->z*D12+n3->z*D13;
    Zx=n1->z*D21+n2->z*D22+n3->z*D23;
    Zy=n1->z*D31+n2->z*D32+n3->z*D33;
    }
  else
    {
    Zo=(n1->z+n2->z+n3->z)/3.;
    Zx=Zy=0.;
    }

/* project light source onto plane of element */

  if(!(Light.a|Light.s))
    Abort(__LINE__,"you must call SetSpotLight() or
    SetAmbientLighting() before rendering");
  w1.x=n2->x-n1->x;
  w1.y=n2->y-n1->y;
  w1.z=n2->z-n1->z;
  w2.x=n3->x-n1->x;
```

```
w2.y=n3->y-n1->y;
w2.z=n3->z-n1->z;
w3.x=w1.y*w2.z-w1.z*w2.y;
w3.y=w1.z*w2.x-w1.x*w2.z;
w3.z=w1.x*w2.y-w1.y*w2.x;
Z=sqrt(w3.x*w3.x+w3.y*w3.y+w3.z*w3.z);
if(Z>DBL_EPSILON)
   {
   w3.x/=Z;
   w3.y/=Z;
   w3.z/=Z;
   }
else
   {
   w3.x=0.;
   w3.y=0.;
   w3.z=0.;
   }
Z=w3.x*Light.n.x+w3.y*Light.n.y+w3.z*Light.n.z;
Z=max(0.,min(1.,fabs(Z)));
g=max(0,min(32,(BYTE)nint(32.*Z)));
s=background?black:white;

/* paint element */

x1=nint(n1->x);
y1=nint(n1->y);
x2=nint(n2->x);
y2=nint(n2->y);
x3=nint(n3->x);
y3=nint(n3->y);

while(1)
   {
   if(y1>y2)
      {
      y=y1;
      y1=y2;
      y2=y;
      x=x1;
      x1=x2;
      x2=x;
      }
   else if(y2>y3)
      {
      y=y2;
      y2=y3;
      y3=y;
      x=x2;
```

45

```
      x2=x3;
      x3=x;
      }
    else
      break;
    }
ya=max(0,y1);
yb=min(y2,Scene.h);
for(y=ya;y<yb;y++)
    {
    if(y1==y2||x1==x2)
      xa=x1;
    else
      xa=(x1*(y2-y)+x2*(y-y1))/(y2-y1);
    if(y1==y3||x1==x3)
      xb=x3;
    else
    xb=(x1*(y3-y)+x3*(y-y1))/(y3-y1);
    if(xa>xb)
      {
      x=xa;
      xa=xb;
      xb=x;
      }
    xa=max(0,xa);
    xb=min(xb,Scene.w-1);
    i=Scene.w*y+xa;
    Z=Zo+Zx*xa+Zy*y;
    for(x=xa;x<=xb;x++,i++,Z+=Zx)
      {
      if(Z<=Scene.z[i])
        continue;
      Scene.z[i]=Z;
      if(show_elements&&(x==xa||x==xb))
        Scene.c[i]=s;
      else if((x+y)%2)
        Scene.c[i]=g;
      else
        Scene.c[i]=c;
      }
    }
ya=max(0,y2);
yb=min(y3,Scene.h-1);
for(y=ya;y<=yb;y++)
    {
    if(y2==y3||x2==x3)
      xa=x2;
    else
      xa=(x2*(y3-y)+x3*(y-y2))/(y3-y2);
```

```
if(y1==y3||x1==x3)
  xb=x3;
else
  xb=(x1*(y3-y)+x3*(y-y1))/(y3-y1);
if(xa>xb)
  {
  x=xa;
  xa=xb;
  xb=x;
  }
xa=max(0,xa);
xb=min(xb,Scene.w-1);
i=Scene.w*y+xa;
Z=Zo+Zx*xa+Zy*y;
for(x=xa;x<=xb;x++,i++,Z+=Zx)
  {
  if(Z<=Scene.z[i])
    continue;
  Scene.z[i]=Z;
  if(show_elements&&(x==xa||x==xb))
    Scene.c[i]=s;
  else if((x+y)%2)
    Scene.c[i]=g;
  else
    Scene.c[i]=c;
  }
}
}
```

Chapter 15. Simple Sort and Paint

A simple way to render 3D objects is to sort them by their distance from the viewer and paint them back to front. The flange example illustrates this technique. It can be fast and can produce acceptable results in many cases, but is rather limited in quality, as illustrated in the following figure:

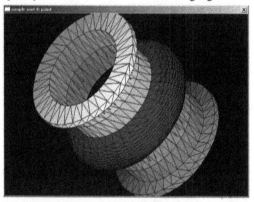

In this example the object is constructed from 3D triangular elements, each with a basic color. When rendering, the three nodes defining each element are rotated, scaled, and centered. The x and y location of each node is converted to an integer, where it will be painted into the display buffer in memory. The base color of each element is modified in brightness, based on the depth (i.e., z location), to enhance the perception of depth.

In this example, all of the drawing and painting is implemented using Windows® API calls. The final result is painted onto the display using BitBlt() to eliminate flicker. This simple orthographic projection could be improved to show perspective.

Note that some of the lines overlap in the figure above. This is due to the fact that all of the elements are painted, regardless of their position, only the order of painting is sorted so that the closer elements are painted last. You could add a check for the orientation of each element and only draw the ones facing the observer.

The sort and paint process is very simple. The sorting process requires only a few lines of code:

```
int CompareDepth(const void*v1,const void*v2)
  {
  return(Elem[*(int*)v1].z-Elem[*(int*)v2].z);
  }
...
  depth=calloc(Ne,sizeof(int));
  for(n=0;n<Ne;n++)
    depth[n]=n;
```

49

```
qsort(depth,Ne,sizeof(int),CompareDepth);
for(n=0;n<Ne;n++)
   {
   i=depth[n];
   rgb=Shade(Elem[i].rgb,Elem[i].z);
   hbr=CreateSolidBrush(rgb);
   hbr=SelectObject(buffer.dc,hbr);
   Polygon(buffer.dc,Elem[i].p,3);
   hbr=SelectObject(buffer.dc,hbr);
   DeleteObject(hbr);
   }
free(depth);
```

The depth index is first filled with the default order, depth[n]=n, then qsort() is used with CompareDepth() to rearrange the order. Finally, the polygons are drawn in the sorted order. The depth index is only needed for these few steps.

The flange example rotates based on a timer. The surface example is quite similar, only it uses a rainbow of colors from blue to red based on elevation. The surface example also accepts keyboard input to control rotation and zoom. Three different surfaces are included. The following is an example:

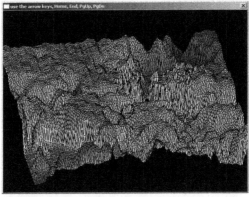

The keyboard input is handled by the following simple section of code:

```
if(wMsg==WM_KEYDOWN)
   {
   if(LOWORD(wParam)==VK_RIGHT)
     angle.x+=5;
   else if(LOWORD(wParam)==VK_LEFT)
     angle.x-=5;
   else if(LOWORD(wParam)==VK_DOWN)
     angle.y+=5;
   else if(LOWORD(wParam)==VK_UP)
     angle.y-=5;
   else if(LOWORD(wParam)==VK_END)
     angle.z+=5;
```

50

```
else if(LOWORD(wParam)==VK_HOME)
  angle.z-=5;
else if(LOWORD(wParam)==VK_PRIOR)
  scale.S*=1.05;
else if(LOWORD(wParam)==VK_NEXT)
  scale.S/=1.05;
else
  return(FALSE);
RenderObjects();
return(FALSE);
}
```

The sombrero surface is included with this example:

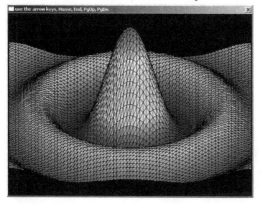

Chapter 16. The Generic 3D Model Viewer

The View3D example illustrates how to import, export, and render general 3D objects without using OpenGL®. It works with 8-bit color and will create animated GIFs. It contains everything you need to accomplish these functions and doesn't depend on any third-party drivers or libraries. The following is typical rendering of a familiar object:

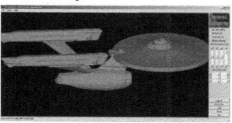

This application also includes the functions to build several geometric shapes, including: chess king, coil, cone, cylinder, disk, dodecahedron, ellipsoid, hexahedron, icosahedron, Klein bottle, octahedron, pipe (or tube), polygon, rectangle, ring, rotoid (meandering tube of varying radius, such as the handle and spout of the teapot), sea shell, sombrero, sphere, teapot, tetrahedron, and torus. The sea shell is shown below:

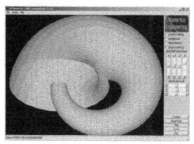

Chapter 17. Virtual Reality Markup Language

Virtual Reality Markup Language (VRML) is used throughout the Internet for creating 3D models and many are available free on-line. I have included a VRML viewer and 9 models of familiar Star Trek® and Star Wars® objects. This 669 line program will read VRML and display the model. It also accepts keyboard input to control rotation and zoom.

The display quality is rather poor, as the simple sort and paint method is used, but you could replace this simple implementation with one of the more complex ones, such as OpenGL®. The most useful part of this code is reading the VRLM. You could also add this section to either View3DS (that uses OpenGL®) or View3D (which uses an 8-bit painting scheme). The short-comings of the sort and paint implementation can be clearly seen in this figure:

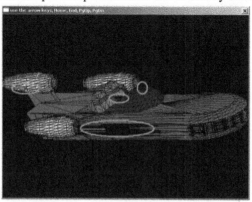

If this model had been rendered with a Z-buffer, the flaws highlighted in the above figure would not be present. Use of perspective and surface texturing (as in the other applications contained herein) would also greatly enhance the appearance, especially of this next model:

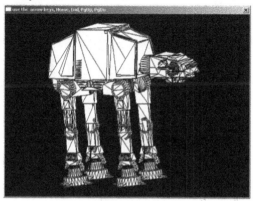

While the 3D Studio® file format is binary, the VRML format is plain ASCII text. There are many documents available on-line describing the VRML format, so the presentation here will be brief. VRML script includes comments, beginning with # and consists of sections, set off by opening and closing braces. The following snippet illustrates transforms, lighting, and material properties:

```
#VRML V1.0 ascii
# Pioneer (tm) was used to create this VRML file.
Separator {
 Background {
  fields [ MFColor skyColors ]
  skyColors    0.502 0.502 0.502
  }
 TransformSeparator {
 MatrixTransform {
  matrix
    1.000 0.000 0.000 0
    0.000 -0.000 -1.000 0
    0.000 1.000 -0.000 0
    4.827 4.089 1.121 1
  }
 }
 Separator {
 MaterialBinding {
  value OVERALL
  }
 Material {
  ambientColor [
    0.300 0.300 0.300,
  ]
  diffuseColor [
    0.604 0.604 0.604,
  ]
  specularColor [
    0.300 0.300 0.300,
  ]
  emissiveColor [
    0.000 0.000 0.000,
  ]
  shininess [
    0.340,
  ]
  transparency [
    0.000,
  ]
  }
  ...
}
```

The model may be broken up into several sections, each with a different transformation and colors. The vertices are defined in a section marked as "coordinates" and the polygons are defined in a section marked as "indices." The orientation of the polygons is also provided, as this is essential for determining the outward normal of the surfaces. The following snippet illustrates the vertices and polygons:

```
Coordinate3 {
  point      [
    -0.578 -0.248 3.625,
    -0.402 -0.248 3.813,
    -0.402 -0.018 3.813,
    -0.578 -0.018 3.625,
    -0.459 -0.248 3.514,
    -0.283 -0.248 3.702,
    -0.283 -0.018 3.702,
    -0.459 -0.018 3.514,
    -0.720 -0.538 3.687,
    0.796 -0.538 3.687,
    0.796 -0.224 3.687,
    -0.720 -0.224 3.687,
    -0.720 -0.538 3.651,
    0.796 -0.538 3.651,
    0.796 -0.224 3.651,
    -0.720 -0.224 3.651,
    -0.351 0.601 3.655,
  ]
}
ShapeHints {
  creaseAngle 0.698
  vertexOrdering CLOCKWISE
  shapeType SOLID
  faceType UNKNOWN_FACE_TYPE
}
DEF City IndexedFaceSet {
  coordIndex [
    2, 1, 0, -1,
    3, 2, 0, -1,
    5, 4, 0, -1,
    1, 5, 0, -1,
    6, 5, 1, -1,
    2, 6, 1, -1,
    7, 6, 2, -1,
    3, 7, 2, -1,
    4, 7, 3, -1,
    0, 4, 3, -1,
    6, 7, 4, -1,
    5, 6, 4, -1,
  ]
```

```
    }
  }
```

The model structure inherent in the VRML format is one that I have found to be most efficient. The VRML View application uses a list of triangles, as this is easily rendered using the Windows® API calls. This is simple to encode, but less efficient. In general, there will be far more elements than nodes in a model. The node transformations may also be more computationally intensive, depending on the speed of the Floating-Point-Unit (FPU). It is, therefore, more efficient to keep the nodes and polygons separate. In the rendering process, first transform all of the nodes in a loop, and then draw all of the polygons, which are simply lists of nodes. In VRML parts of the model may be described separately and you may want to keep this distinction, rather than combining all of the parts.

As illustrated in the preceding script snippets, the structure of VRML is simple and straightforward, making it relatively easy to understand and read. The following code performs this task:

```
char*getwrl(char*bufr,FILE*fp)
  {
  int i,l=0;
  while(1)
    {
    i=fgetc(fp);
    if(i==EOF)
      {
      if(l)
        {
        bufr[l]=0;
        return(bufr);
        }
      else
        return(NULL);
      }
    else if(i<=' '||i==',')
      {
      if(l)
        {
        bufr[l]=0;
        return(bufr);
        }
      }
    else if(strchr("{[]}",i))
      {
      if(l)
        {
        ungetc(i,fp);
        bufr[l]=0;
        return(bufr);
        }
```

```
    else
      {
      bufr[0]=i;
      bufr[1]=0;
      return(bufr);
      }
    }
  else
    bufr[l++]=i;
  }
}

struct{int*index,m,n;}poly;
struct{DWORD*rgb;int m,n;}matl;
typedef struct{double X,Y,Z;}XYZ;
struct{XYZ*xyz;int m,n;}node;

void AddPoly(int i,int j,int k,DWORD rgb)
  {
  XYZ p,q,r;
  p=node.xyz[poly.index[i]];
  q=node.xyz[poly.index[j]];
  r=node.xyz[poly.index[k]];
  AddTriangle(p.X,-p.Z,-p.Y,q.X,-q.Z,-q.Y,r.X,-r.Z,-
    r.Y,rgb);
  }

void ReadVRML(char*fname)
  {
  char bufr[128],*ptr;
  int ccw=TRUE,MaterialBinding=FALSE;
  int b,g,i,j,m,n,r;
  double B,G,R,X,Y,Z;
  FILE*fp;

  if((fp=fopen(fname,"rt"))==NULL)
    Abort(__LINE__,"can't open file %s",fname);

  matl.m=100;
  matl.n=0;
  matl.rgb=allocate(__LINE__,matl.m,sizeof(DWORD));
  matl.rgb[0]=0xFF0000;

  node.m=1000;
  node.n=0;
  node.xyz=allocate(__LINE__,node.m,sizeof(XYZ));

  poly.m=1000;
  poly.n=0;
```

59

```
poly.index=allocate(__LINE__,poly.m,sizeof(int));

while((ptr=getwrl(bufr,fp))!=NULL)
  {
  if(!_stricmp(ptr,"ccw"))
    {
    if((ptr=getwrl(bufr,fp))==NULL)
      Abort(__LINE__,"unexpected EOF");
    if(!_stricmp(ptr,"FALSE"))
      ccw=FALSE;
    else if(!_stricmp(ptr,"TRUE"))
      ccw=TRUE;
    else if(_stricmp(ptr,"UNKNOWN"))
      Abort(__LINE__,"expected ccw to be TRUE or
  FALSE");
    }
  else if(!_stricmp(ptr,"colorIndex"))
    Abort(__LINE__,"can't handle colorIndex yet");//
  else if(!_stricmp(ptr,"coordIndex"))
    {
    if(node.n==0)
      Abort(__LINE__,"points expected before
  coordIndex");
    if((ptr=getwrl(bufr,fp))==NULL)
      Abort(__LINE__,"unexpected EOF");
    if(strcmp(ptr,"\x5B"))
      Abort(__LINE__,"expected \x5B to follow
  coordIndex");
    poly.n=0;
    while(1)
      {
      if((ptr=getwrl(bufr,fp))==NULL)
        Abort(__LINE__,"unexpected EOF");
      if(!strcmp(ptr,"\x5D"))
        break;
      if(sscanf(ptr,"%li",&n)!=1)
        Abort(__LINE__,"scan error");
      if(n>=node.n)
        Abort(__LINE__,"no such point %li",n);
      if(poly.n>=poly.m)
        {
        poly.m+=1000;
        poly.index=reallocate(__LINE__,poly.index,
  poly.n,poly.m,sizeof(int));
        }
      poly.index[poly.n++]=n;
      }
    if(MaterialBinding)
      continue;
```

```
    i=0;
    while(i<poly.n)
        {
        n=0;
        while(poly.index[i+n]>=0)
          n++;
        if(ccw)
          for(j=2;j<n;j++)
            AddPoly(i+j-2,i+j-1,i+j,matl.rgb[0]);
        else
          for(j=2;j<n;j++)
            AddPoly(i+j,i+j-1,i+j-2,matl.rgb[0]);
        i+=n+1;
        }
    poly.n=0;
    }
  else if(!_stricmp(ptr,"diffuseColor"))
    {
    if((ptr=getwrl(bufr,fp))==NULL)
      Abort(__LINE__,"unexpected EOF");
    matl.n=n=0;
    matl.rgb[0]=0xFF0000;
    if(strcmp(ptr,"\x5B"))
      n=1;
    while(1)
      {
      if(n==0)
        {
        if((ptr=getwrl(bufr,fp))==NULL)
          Abort(__LINE__,"unexpected EOF");
        if(!strcmp(ptr,"\x5D"))
          break;
        }
      if(sscanf(ptr,"%lf",&R)!=1)
        Abort(__LINE__,"scan error");
      if((ptr=getwrl(bufr,fp))==NULL)
        Abort(__LINE__,"unexpected EOF");
      if(sscanf(ptr,"%lf",&G)!=1)
        Abort(__LINE__,"scan error");
      if((ptr=getwrl(bufr,fp))==NULL)
        Abort(__LINE__,"unexpected EOF");
      if(sscanf(ptr,"%lf",&B)!=1)
        Abort(__LINE__,"scan error");
      if(matl.n>=matl.m)
        {
        matl.m+=100;
        matl.rgb=reallocate(__LINE__,matl.rgb,matl.n,
matl.m,sizeof(DWORD));
        }
```

```
            r=(BYTE)max(0,min(255,255*R));
            g=(BYTE)max(0,min(255,255*G));
            b=(BYTE)max(0,min(255,255*B));
            matl.rgb[matl.n++]=RGB(r,g,b);
            if(n!=0)
               break;
            }
         }
      else if(!_stricmp(ptr,"MaterialBinding"))
         {
         if((ptr=getwrl(bufr,fp))==NULL)
            Abort(__LINE__,"unexpected EOF");
         if(strcmp(ptr,"\x7B"))
            Abort(__LINE__,"expected \x7B to follow
      MaterialBinding");
         if((ptr=getwrl(bufr,fp))==NULL)
            Abort(__LINE__,"unexpected EOF");
         if(_stricmp(ptr,"value"))
            Abort(__LINE__,"expected value to follow
      MaterialBinding");
         if((ptr=getwrl(bufr,fp))==NULL)
            Abort(__LINE__,"unexpected EOF");
         if(!_stricmp(ptr,"OVERALL"))
            MaterialBinding=FALSE;
         else if(stristr(ptr,"PER_FACE_INDEXED"))
            MaterialBinding=TRUE;
         else if(!_stricmp(ptr,"PER_FACE"))
            MaterialBinding=TRUE;
         else
            Abort(__LINE__,"expected OVERALL, PER_FACE, or
      PER_FACE_INDEXED MaterialBinding");
         if((ptr=getwrl(bufr,fp))==NULL)
            Abort(__LINE__,"unexpected EOF");
         if(strcmp(ptr,"\x7D"))
            Abort(__LINE__,"expected \x7D to follow
      MaterialBinding");
         }
      else if(!_stricmp(ptr,"materialIndex"))
         {
         if(poly.n==0)
            Abort(__LINE__,"coordIndex expected before
      materialIndex");
         if((ptr=getwrl(bufr,fp))==NULL)
            Abort(__LINE__,"unexpected EOF");
         if(strcmp(ptr,"\x5B"))
            Abort(__LINE__,"expected \x5B to follow
      materialIndex");
         i=0;
         while(1)
```

```c
      {
      if((ptr=getwrl(bufr,fp))==NULL)
        Abort(__LINE__,"unexpected EOF");
      if(!strcmp(ptr,"\x5D"))
        break;
      if(sscanf(ptr,"%li",&m)!=1)
        Abort(__LINE__,"scan error");
      if(m<0||m>=matl.n)
        Abort(__LINE__,"no such material %li",m);
      if(i>=poly.n)
        Abort(__LINE__,"more material indices than
coordIndex groups");
      n=0;
      while(poly.index[i+n]>=0)
        n++;
      if(ccw)
        for(j=2;j<n;j++)
          AddPoly(i+j-2,i+j-1,i+j,matl.rgb[0]);
      else
        for(j=2;j<n;j++)
          AddPoly(i+j,i+j-1,i+j-2,matl.rgb[0]);
      i+=n+1;
      }
   if(i<poly.n)
     Abort(__LINE__,"fewer material indices than
coordIndex groups");
   poly.n=0;
   }
 else if(!_stricmp(ptr,"point"))
   {
   if((ptr=getwrl(bufr,fp))==NULL)
     Abort(__LINE__,"unexpected EOF");
   if(strcmp(ptr,"\x5B"))
     Abort(__LINE__,"expected \x5B to follow point");
   node.n=0;
   while(1)
     {
     if((ptr=getwrl(bufr,fp))==NULL)
       Abort(__LINE__,"unexpected EOF");
     if(!strcmp(ptr,"\x5D"))
       break;
     if(sscanf(ptr,"%lf",&X)!=1)
       Abort(__LINE__,"scan error");
     if((ptr=getwrl(bufr,fp))==NULL)
       Abort(__LINE__,"unexpected EOF");
     if(sscanf(ptr,"%lf",&Y)!=1)
       Abort(__LINE__,"scan error");
     if((ptr=getwrl(bufr,fp))==NULL)
       Abort(__LINE__,"unexpected EOF");
```

```c
      if(sscanf(ptr,"%lf",&Z)!=1)
        Abort(__LINE__,"scan error");
      if(node.n>=node.m)
        {
        node.m+=1000;
        node.xyz=reallocate(__LINE__,node.xyz,node.n,
  node.m,sizeof(XYZ));
        }
      node.xyz[node.n].X=X;
      node.xyz[node.n].Y=Y;
      node.xyz[node.n].Z=Z;
      node.n++;
      }
    }
  else if(!_stricmp(ptr,"vertexOrdering"))
    {
    if((ptr=getwrl(bufr,fp))==NULL)
      Abort(__LINE__,"unexpected EOF");
    if(!_stricmp(ptr,"CLOCKWISE"))
      ccw=FALSE;
    else if(!_stricmp(ptr,"COUNTERCLOCKWISE"))
      ccw=TRUE;
    else if(_stricmp(ptr,"UNKNOWN_ORDERING"))
      Abort(__LINE__,"expected vertexOrdering to be
  CLOCKWISE or COUNTERCLOCKWISE");
    }
  }

fclose(fp);

free(poly.index);
free(matl.rgb);
free(node.xyz);
}
```

Chapter 18. Sky Fly

The Sky Fly example is perhaps the most complicated example included in the archive. It incorporates scene rendering (terrain and sky), a constantly changing viewer location, and complex mouse interaction. There are also "sprites" (little yellow paper airplanes) that fly about. The speed with which the scene is rendered is impressive. Mastering this example is a must for the advanced developer, especially if gaming is your objective.

The sprites are created with the following structures and functions:

```
/*This is the structure which contains the database. It
   is amalloc'ed
 *in shared memory so that forked processes can access
   it. Notice how
 *the flags and vertex data are separated to improve
   cacheing behavior.
 */
typedef struct shared_data_struct {
  /* objects */
  perfobj_t paper_plane_obj;
  perfobj_t paper_plane_start_obj;
  perfobj_t paper_plane_2ndpass_obj;
  perfobj_t paper_plane_end_obj;
  perfobj_t terrain_texture_obj;
  perfobj_t*terrain_cells;
  perfobj_t clouds_texture_obj;
  perfobj_t clouds_obj;
  /* flags */
  unsigned int paper_plane_flags[2];
  unsigned int paper_plane_start_flags[3];
  unsigned int paper_plane_2ndpass_flags[3];
  unsigned int paper_plane_end_flags[3];
  unsigned int terrain_texture_flags[3];
  unsigned int**terrain_cell_flags;
```

```
  unsigned int clouds_texture_flags[3];
  unsigned int clouds_flags[2];
  /* data */
  perfobj_vert_t paper_plane_verts[22];
  perfobj_vert_t**terrain_cell_verts;
  perfobj_vert_t clouds_verts[4];
  }shared_data;

/* perfobj flags */
#define PD_TEXTURE_BIND         0
#define PD_DRAW_PAPER_PLANE      1
#define PD_DRAW_TERRAIN_CELL     2
#define PD_PAPER_PLANE_MODE      3
#define PD_PAPER_PLANE_POS       4
#define PD_VIEWER_POS            5
#define PD_DRAW_CLOUDS           6
#define PD_END                  0x3fff
#define PLANES_START             0
#define PLANES_SECOND_PASS       1
#define PLANES_END               2

/* Offsets to data in perfobj_vert_t */
#define PD_V_POINT     0
#define PD_V_CPACK     3
#define PD_V_NORMAL    4
#define PD_V_COLOR     8
#define PD_V_TEX       12
#define PD_V_SIZE      16

void put_paper_plane(float*source,perfobj_t*pobj)
  {
  int j;
  perfobj_vert_t*pdataptr=(perfobj_vert_t*)pobj->vdata;
  unsigned int*flagsptr=pobj->flags;
  float*sp=source;
  *flagsptr++=PD_DRAW_PAPER_PLANE;
  for(j=0;j<22;j++)
    {
    putn3fdata(sp+0,pdataptr);
    putv3fdata(sp+3,pdataptr);
    sp+=6;
    pdataptr++;
    }
  *flagsptr++=PD_END;
  }

void init_paper_planes(void)
  {
  perfobj_t*pobj;
```

```
/* create various perf-objs for planes */
pobj=&(SharedData->paper_plane_obj);
pobj->flags=SharedData->paper_plane_flags;
pobj->vdata=(float*)SharedData->paper_plane_verts;
put_paper_plane(paper_plane_vertexes,pobj);
pobj=&(SharedData->paper_plane_start_obj);
pobj->flags=SharedData->paper_plane_start_flags;
*(pobj->flags)=PD_PAPER_PLANE_MODE;
*(pobj->flags+1)=PLANES_START;
*(pobj->flags+2)=PD_END;
pobj=&(SharedData->paper_plane_2ndpass_obj);
pobj->flags=SharedData->paper_plane_2ndpass_flags;
*(pobj->flags)=PD_PAPER_PLANE_MODE;
*(pobj->flags+1)=PLANES_SECOND_PASS;
*(pobj->flags+2)=PD_END;
pobj=&(SharedData->paper_plane_end_obj);
pobj->flags=SharedData->paper_plane_end_flags;
*(pobj->flags)=PD_PAPER_PLANE_MODE;
*(pobj->flags+1)=PLANES_END;
*(pobj->flags+2)=PD_END;
}

void fly_paper_planes(perfobj_t*paper_plane_pos)
{
int i;
float speed=.08;
float terrain_z;
/* slow planes down in cyclops mode since frame rate
  is doubled */
for(i=0;i<NUM_PLANES;i++)
  {
  /* If plane is not turning,one chance in 50 of
  starting a turn */
  if(flock[i].Pcount==0 && IRND(50)==1)
    {
    /* initiate a roll */
    /* roll for a random period */
    flock[i].Pcount=IRND(100);
    /* random turn rate */
    flock[i].Pturn_rate=IRND(100)/10000.;
    flock[i].Pdirection=IRND(3)-1;
    }
  if(flock[i].Pcount>0)
    {
    /* continue rolling */
    flock[i].Proll+=flock[i].Pdirection*
  flock[i].Pturn_rate;
    flock[i].Pcount--;
    }
```

```
      else
       /* damp amount of roll when turn complete */
       flock[i].Proll*=.95;
      /* turn as a function of roll */
      flock[i].Pazimuth-=flock[i].Proll*.05;
      /* follow terrain elevation */
      terrain_z=terrain_height(flock[i].PX,flock[i].PY);
      /* use a "spring-mass-damp" system of terrain follow
      */
      flock[i].PZv=flock[i].PZv -
       .01*(flock[i].PZ-(max(terrain_z,0.) +
       2.*(float) i/NUM_PLANES+.3))-flock[i].PZv*.04;
      /* U-turn if fly off world!! */
      if(flock[i].PX<1||flock[i].PX>GRID_RANGE-
    2||flock[i].PY<1||flock[i].PY>GRID_RANGE-2)
        flock[i].Pazimuth+=M_PI;
      /* move planes */
      flock[i].PX+=cosf(flock[i].Pazimuth)*speed;
      flock[i].PY+=sinf(flock[i].Pazimuth)*speed;
      flock[i].PZ+=flock[i].PZv;
      }
    for(i=0;i<NUM_PLANES;i++)
      {
      *((float*)paper_plane_pos[i].vdata+0)=flock[i].PX;
      *((float*)paper_plane_pos[i].vdata+1)=flock[i].PY;
      *((float*)paper_plane_pos[i].vdata+2)=flock[i].PZ;
      *((float*)paper_plane_pos[i].vdata+3)
    =flock[i].Pazimuth*RAD_TO_DEG;
      *((float*)paper_plane_pos[i].vdata+4)
    =flock[i].PZv*(-500.);
      *((float*)paper_plane_pos[i].vdata+5)
    =flock[i].Proll*RAD_TO_DEG;
      }
    }
```

The terrain is created, eroded (to make it look more like rolling hills), and colored (to make it look like grass and dirt), by the following code:

```
void create_terrain(void)
  {
  int r,c,i,x1,y1,x2,y2;
  int hillsize;
  hillsize=GRID_RANGE/12;
  A=(float*)calloc(GridDim*GridDim,sizeof(float));
  /* initialize elevation to zero,except band down
    middle where make a maximum height 'hill' that will
    later be inverted to
  *make the negative elevation 'canyon' */
  for(r=0;r<GridDim;r++)
    for(c=0;c<GridDim;c++)
```

```
    if(r>=(GridDim/2-2-IRND(2)) &&
 r<=(GridDim/2+2+IRND(2)))
        A[r*GridDim+c]=1.0;
    else
        A[r*GridDim+c]=0.0;
/* create random sinusoidal hills that add on top of
 each other */
for(i=1;i<=10*GridDim;i++)
  {
  /* randomly position hill */
  x1=IRND(GridDim-hillsize);
  x2=x1+hillsize/8+IRND(hillsize-hillsize/8);
  y1=IRND(GridDim-hillsize);
  y2=y1+hillsize/8+IRND(hillsize-hillsize/8);
  if((x1<=GridDim/2-4 && x2>=GridDim/2-4) ||
   (x1<=GridDim/2+4 && x2>=GridDim/2+4))
    {
    x1=IRND(2)-2+GridDim/2;
    x2=x1+IRND(GridDim/2-x1+2);
    }
  /* make a sinusoidal hill */
  for(r=x1;r<x2;r++)
    for(c=y1;c<y2;c++)
      {
      A[r*GridDim+c]+=.35 *
       (sinf(M_PI*(float)(r-x1)/(float)(x2-x1)) *
       (sinf(M_PI*(float)(c-y1)/(float)(y2-y1)))));
      }
  }
/* clamp the elevation of the terrain */
for(r=1;r<GridDim;r++)
  for(c=1;c<GridDim;c++)
    {
    A[r*GridDim+c]=min(A[r*GridDim+c],.95);
    A[r*GridDim+c]=max(A[r*GridDim+c],0.);
    }
}

#define NUM_DROPS 80

void erode_terrain(void)
  {
  float x,y,xv,yv,dx,dy;
  float cut,min,take;
  int nm;
  static int t,xi,yi,xo,yo,done;
  int ii,jj,r,c;
  for(nm=1;nm<NUM_DROPS*GridDim;nm++)
    {
```

```
/* find a random position to start the 'rain drop'
*/
x=(float)(IRND(GridDim));
y=(float)(IRND(GridDim));
/* Clamp x and y to be inside grid */
x=min(max(2.,x),(float) GridDim-2.);
y=min(max(2.,y),(float) GridDim-2.);
done=0;
yv=xv=0.;
t=0;
cut=.3;
while(!done)
  {
  xi=(int) x;
  yi=(int) y;
  min=90.;
  if(xi!=xo||yi!=yo)
    {
    cut*=.99;
    /* gradient */
    dx=(A[(xi+1)*GridDim+yi]-A[(xi-1)*GridDim+yi]);
    dy=(A[xi*GridDim+yi+1]-A[xi*GridDim+yi-1]);
    /* find lowest neighbor */
    for(ii=-1;ii<=1;ii++)
      for(jj=-1;jj<=1;jj++)
        if(A[(xi+ii)*GridDim+yi+jj]<min)
          min=A[(xi+ii)*GridDim+yi+jj];
    /* evaporate drop if sitting on my old location
*/
    if(M[xi][yi]==nm)
      done=1;
    M[xi][yi]=nm;
    /* cave in neighbors by .3 */
    for(ii=-1;ii<=1;ii++)
      for(jj=-1;jj<=1;jj++)
        {
        take=.3*cut*(A[(xi+ii)*GridDim+yi+jj]-min);
        A[(xi+ii)*GridDim+yi+jj]-=take;
        }
    /* take away from this cell by .7 */
    take=(A[xi*GridDim+yi]-min)*.7*cut;
    A[xi*GridDim+yi]-=take;
    }
  xo=xi;
  yo=yi;
  /* move drop using kinematic motion */
  xv=xv-dx-.8*xv;
  yv=yv-dy-.8*yv;
  x+=xv;
```

```
      y+=yv;
      /* make sure can't move by more that 1.0 in any
   direction */
      xv=max(xv,-1);
      yv=max(yv,-1);
      xv=min(xv,1);
      yv=min(yv,1);
      /* check to see if need a new drop */
      /* ie ran of world,got stuck,or at 'sea level' */
      if(x<1.||x>GridDim-1.||y<1.||y>GridDim-1.
      ||t++>2000
      ||cut<.01)
        done=1;
      if(A[xi*GridDim+yi]<0.0001)
        {
        A[xi*GridDim+yi]=0.;
        done=1;
        }
      } /* while(!done) with this drop */
   } /* next drop */
   /* invert the pseudo hill int the pseudo canyon */
   for(r=0;r<GridDim;r++)
     for(c=0;c<GridDim;c++)
       if(r>=GridDim/2-4 && r<=GridDim/2+4)
         A[r*GridDim+c]=max((-3.2*A[r*GridDim+c]),-1.8);
   }

void color_terrain(void)
   {
   float N[3],D,alt,maxelev=-1.;
   int x,y;
   for(x=0;x<GridDim;x++)
     for(y=0;y<GridDim;y++)
       maxelev=max(maxelev,A[x*GridDim+y]);
   for(x=1;x<GridDim-1;x++)
     for(y=1;y<GridDim-1;y++)
       {
       alt=A[x*GridDim+y]*1.5;
       /* randomly perterb to get a mottling effect */
       alt+=IRND(100)/400.-.125;
       alt=min(alt,1.0);
       if(alt<-.11)
         {
         C[x][y][0]=0.6;/* soil/rock in canyon */
         C[x][y][1]=0.5;
         C[x][y][2]=0.2;
         }
       else if(alt<.000001)
         {
```

```
        C[x][y][0]=0.0;/* dark,jungle lowlands */
        C[x][y][1]=0.2;
        C[x][y][2]=0.05;
        }
      else if(alt<.90)
        {
        C[x][y][0]=alt*.25;/* green to redish hillsides
*/
        C[x][y][1]=(1.0-alt)*.4+.1;
        C[x][y][2]=0.1;
        }
      else
        {
        C[x][y][0]=alt;
        C[x][y][1]=alt;/* incresingly white snow */
        C[x][y][2]=alt;
        }
      /* compute normal to terrain */
      N[0]=A[(x-1)*GridDim+y]-A[(x+1)*GridDim+y];
      N[1]=A[x*GridDim+y-1]-A[x*GridDim+y+1];
      N[2]=2.0/ScaleZ;
      D=1.0/sqrtf(N[0]*N[0]+N[1]*N[1]+N[2]*N[2]);
      N[0]*=D;
      N[1]*=D;
      N[2]*=D;
      /* perform diffuse lighting of terrain */
      D=N[0]*LX+N[1]*LY+N[2]*LZ;
      D*=1.2;
      if(!IRND(4))
        D*=.5;
      D=max(D,0);
      /* darken terrain on shaded side */
      C[x][y][0]*=D;
      C[x][y][1]*=D;
      C[x][y][2]*=D;
      S[x][y]=(float)(x)/(float) CellDim;
      T[x][y]=(float)(y)/(float) CellDim;
      }
  }
```

The sky is created by the following functions:

```
void put_clouds_vert(float s,float t,float x,float
  y,float z,perfobj_vert_t*pdataptr)
  {
  float D[5];
  D[0]=s;
  D[1]=t;
  D[2]=x;
  D[3]=y;
  D[4]=z;
```

```
  putt2fdata(D,pdataptr);
  putv3fdata(D+2,pdataptr);
  }
void init_clouds(void)
  {
  perfobj_t*pobj;
  perfobj_vert_t*pdataptr;
  clouds=0;
  pobj=&(SharedData->clouds_texture_obj);
  pobj->flags=SharedData->clouds_texture_flags;
  put_texture_bind(2,pobj);
  pobj=&(SharedData->clouds_obj);
  pobj->flags=SharedData->clouds_flags;
  pobj->vdata=(float*)SharedData->clouds_verts;
  *(pobj->flags+0)=PD_DRAW_CLOUDS;
  *(pobj->flags+1)=PD_END;
  pdataptr=(perfobj_vert_t*)pobj->vdata;
  put_clouds_vert(0.,0.,-SKY,-SKY,SKY_HIGH,pdataptr);
  pdataptr++;
  put_clouds_vert(24.,0.,SKY+GRID_RANGE,-
    SKY,SKY_HIGH,pdataptr);
  pdataptr++;
  put_clouds_vert(24.,24.,SKY+GRID_RANGE,
    SKY+GRID_RANGE,SKY_HIGH,pdataptr);
  pdataptr++;
  put_clouds_vert(0.,24.,-
    SKY,SKY+GRID_RANGE,SKY_HIGH,pdataptr);
  }
```

The perception of flying is implemented with the following code:

```
void fly(perfobj_t*viewer_pos)
  {
  float terrain_z,xpos,ypos,xcntr,ycntr;
  float delta_speed=.003;
  xcntr=Wxsize/2;
  ycntr=Wysize/2;
  if(Xgetbutton(RKEY))
    init_positions();
  if(Xgetbutton(SPACEKEY))
    Keyboard_mode=!Keyboard_mode;
  if(Keyboard_mode)
    {
    /* step-at-a-time debugging mode */
    if(Keyboard_mode && Xgetbutton(LEFTARROWKEY))
      Azimuth-=0.025;
    if(Keyboard_mode && Xgetbutton(RIGHTARROWKEY))
      Azimuth+=0.025;
    if(Keyboard_mode && Xgetbutton(UPARROWKEY))
      {
      X+=cosf(-Azimuth+M_PI/2.)*0.025;
```

73

```
        Y+=sinf(-Azimuth+M_PI/2.)*0.025;
        }
    if(Keyboard_mode && Xgetbutton(DOWNARROWKEY))
        {
        X-=cosf(-Azimuth+M_PI/2.)*0.025;
        Y-=sinf(-Azimuth+M_PI/2.)*0.025;
        }
    if(Keyboard_mode && Xgetbutton(PAGEUPKEY))
        Z+=0.025;
    if(Keyboard_mode && Xgetbutton(PAGEDOWNKEY))
        Z-=0.025;
    }
else
    {
    /* simple,mouse-driven flight model */
    if(Xgetbutton(LEFTMOUSE) && Speed<.3)
        Speed+=delta_speed;
    if(Xgetbutton(RIGHTMOUSE) && Speed>-.3)
        Speed-=delta_speed;
    if(Xgetbutton(MIDDLEMOUSE))
        Speed=Speed*.8;
    xpos=(Xgetvaluator(MOUSEX)-xcntr)/((float)
    Wxsize*14.);
    ypos=(Xgetvaluator(MOUSEY)-ycntr)/((float)
    Wysize*.5);
    /* move in direction of view */
    Azimuth+=xpos;
    X+=cosf(-Azimuth+M_PI/2.)*Speed;
    Y+=sinf(-Azimuth+M_PI/2.)*Speed;
    Z-=ypos*Speed;
    }
/* keep from getting too close to terrain */
terrain_z=terrain_height(X,Y);
if(Z<terrain_z+.4)
    Z=terrain_z+.4;
X=max(X,1.);
X=min(X,GRID_RANGE);
Y=max(Y,1.);
Y=min(Y,GRID_RANGE);
Z=min(Z,20.);
*((float*) viewer_pos->vdata+0)=X;
*((float*)viewer_pos->vdata+1)=Y;
*((float*)viewer_pos->vdata+2)=Z;
*((float*)viewer_pos->vdata+3)=Azimuth;
}
```

In this example the speed of rendering is greatly improved by eliminating the objects that aren't visible before passing them to OpenGL®, that is, culling. The following code accomplishes this:

```
void cull_proc(void)
  {
  static struct cull
    {
    perfobj_t**cells;
    perfobj_t viewer_pos_obj[2];
    unsigned int viewer_pos_flags[4];
    float viewer_position[2][4];
    float fovx,side,farr,epsilon,plane_epsilon;
    } cull;
  static int init=0;
  if(!init)
    {
    int x,y;
    cull.fovx=FOV*(float) Wxsize/(float) Wysize;
    cull.side=far_cull/cosf(cull.fovx/2.);
    cull.farr=2.*cull.side*sinf(cull.fovx/2.);
    cull.epsilon=sqrtf(2.)*CellSize/2.;
    cull.plane_epsilon=.5;
    cull.cells=(perfobj_t**)
    malloc(NumCells*NumCells*sizeof(perfobj_t *));
    for(x=0;x<NumCells;x++)
      for(y=0;y<NumCells;y++)
        cull.cells[x*NumCells+y] =
        &(SharedData->terrain_cells[x*NumCells+y]);
    ringbuffer.ring=malloc(RING_SIZE*sizeof(perfobj_t
    *));
    ringbuffer.head=ringbuffer.tail=0;
    cull.viewer_pos_obj[0].flags=cull.viewer_pos_flags;
    cull.viewer_pos_obj[0].vdata=
    cull.viewer_position[0];
    cull.viewer_pos_obj[1].flags=cull.viewer_pos_flags;
    cull.viewer_pos_obj[1].vdata=
    cull.viewer_position[1];
    *(cull.viewer_pos_flags)=PD_VIEWER_POS;
    *(cull.viewer_pos_flags+1)=PD_END;
    init=1;
    }
    {
    float*viewer;
    float vX,vY,vazimuth,px,py;
    float left_area,right_area;
    float left_dx,left_dy,right_dx,right_dy;
    float ax,ay,bx,by,cx,cy;
    float minx,maxx,miny,maxy;
    int i,buffer=0;
    int x,y,x0,y0,x1,y1;
    perfobj_t*viewer_pos, *paper_plane_pos;
    buffered_data*buffered;
```

```
perfobj_t*terrain_texture=&(SharedData-
>terrain_texture_obj);
perfobj_t*paper_plane=&(SharedData-
>paper_plane_obj);
perfobj_t*paper_plane_start=&(SharedData-
>paper_plane_start_obj);
perfobj_t*paper_plane_end=&(SharedData-
>paper_plane_end_obj);
perfobj_t*clouds_texture=&(SharedData-
>clouds_texture_obj);
perfobj_t*clouds=&(SharedData->clouds_obj);
buffered=gfxpipe->buffers[buffer];
viewer_pos=&(buffered->viewer_pos_obj);
paper_plane_pos=buffered->paper_plane_pos_obj;
vX=*((float*)viewer_pos->vdata+0);
vY=*((float*)viewer_pos->vdata+1);
vazimuth=*((float*)viewer_pos->vdata+3);
viewer=cull.viewer_position[buffer];
viewer[0]=vX;
viewer[1]=vY;
viewer[2]=*((float*)viewer_pos->vdata+2);
viewer[3]=vazimuth;
/* Begin cull to viewing frustrum */
ax=(vX-sinf(-vazimuth+cull.fovx*.5)*cull.side);
ay=(vY+cosf(-vazimuth+cull.fovx*.5)*cull.side);
bx=vX;
by=vY;
cx=(vX+sinf(vazimuth+cull.fovx*.5)*cull.side);
cy=(vY+cosf(vazimuth+cull.fovx*.5)*cull.side);
minx=min(min(ax,bx),cx);
miny=min(min(ay,by),cy);
maxx=max(max(ax,bx),cx);
maxy=max(max(ay,by),cy);
x0=max((int)(minx/CellSize),0);
x1=min((int)(maxx/CellSize)+1,NumCells);
y0=max((int)(miny/CellSize),0);
y1=min((int)(maxy/CellSize)+1,NumCells);
left_dx=ax-bx;
left_dy=ay-by;
right_dx=cx-bx;
right_dy=cy-by;
enter_in_ring(&cull.viewer_pos_obj[buffer]);
if(viewer[2]<SKY_HIGH)
    {
    /* draw clouds first */
    enter_in_ring(clouds_texture);
    enter_in_ring(clouds);
    }
enter_in_ring(terrain_texture);
```

```
    /* Add visible cells to ring buffer */
    for(x=x0;x<x1;x++)
       {
       for(y=y0;y<y1;y++)
          {
          float cntrx=(x+.5)*CellSize;
          float cntry=(y+.5)*CellSize;
          left_area=left_dx*(cntry-by)-left_dy*(cntrx-bx);
          right_area=right_dx*(cntry-by)-right_dy*(cntrx-
bx);
          if((left_area<cull.epsilon*cull.side &&
right_area>-cull.epsilon*cull.side))
             {
             enter_in_ring(cull.cells[x*NumCells+y]);
             }
          }
       }
    enter_in_ring(paper_plane_start);
    /* Add visible planes to ring buffer */
    for(i=0;i<NUM_PLANES;i++)
       {
       px=*((float*)paper_plane_pos[i].vdata+0);
       py=*((float*)paper_plane_pos[i].vdata+1);
       left_area=left_dx*(py-by)-left_dy*(px-bx);
       right_area=right_dx*(py-by)-right_dy*(px-bx);
       if(left_area<cull.plane_epsilon*cull.side &&
right_area>-cull.plane_epsilon*cull.side)
          {
          enter_in_ring(&paper_plane_pos[i]);
          enter_in_ring(paper_plane);
          }
       }
    enter_in_ring(paper_plane_end);
    if(viewer[2]>SKY_HIGH)
       {
       /* draw clouds after everything else */
       enter_in_ring(clouds_texture);
       enter_in_ring(clouds);
       }
    enter_in_ring((perfobj_t*)0);/* 0 indicates end of
    frame */
    buffer=!buffer;
    }
 }

/*---------------------------------- Draw ----------
 --------------------*/

void putv3fdata(float*v,perfobj_vert_t*ptr)
```

77

```
  {
  ptr->vert[0]=v[0];
  ptr->vert[1]=v[1];
  ptr->vert[2]=v[2];
  }

void putc3fdata(float*c,perfobj_vert_t*ptr)
  {
  ptr->color[0]=c[0];
  ptr->color[1]=c[1];
  ptr->color[2]=c[2];
  }

void putn3fdata(float*n,perfobj_vert_t*ptr)
  {
  ptr->normal[0]=n[0];
  ptr->normal[1]=n[1];
  ptr->normal[2]=n[2];
  }

void putt2fdata(float*t,perfobj_vert_t*ptr)
  {
  ptr->texture[0]=t[0];
  ptr->texture[1]=t[1];
  }

perfobj_t*get_from_ring(void)
  {
  static perfobj_t*pobj;
  while(ringbuffer.tail==ringbuffer.head)
    ;
  pobj=ringbuffer.ring[ringbuffer.tail%RING_SIZE];
  ringbuffer.tail++;
  return pobj;
  }

void draw_proc(void)
  {
  perfobj_t*too_draw;
  glClear(GL_COLOR_BUFFER_BIT|GL_DEPTH_BUFFER_BIT);
  while((too_draw=get_from_ring()))
    drawperfobj(too_draw);
  }

void draw(void)
  {
  int newCount;
  char buf[20];
  int i,len;
```

```
/* Draw the frame */
cull_proc();
draw_proc();
/* Update the frames per second count if we have gone
   past at least a quarter of a second since the last
   update. */
newCount=glutGet(GLUT_ELAPSED_TIME);
frameCount++;
if((newCount-lastCount)>1000)
  {
  fpsRate=(int)((10000.0F/(newCount-
  lastCount))*frameCount);
  lastCount=newCount;
  frameCount=0;
  }
if(show_timer)
  {
  sprintf(buf,"%3d.%d fps",fpsRate/10,fpsRate%10);
  glPushAttrib(GL_ENABLE_BIT|GL_CURRENT_BIT);
  glDisable(GL_LIGHTING);
  glDisable(GL_TEXTURE_2D);
  glDisable(GL_DEPTH_TEST);
  glDisable(GL_FOG);
  glDisable(GL_BLEND);
  glMatrixMode(GL_PROJECTION);
  glPushMatrix();
  glLoadIdentity();
  glOrtho(0,Wxsize,0,Wysize,-1,1);
  glMatrixMode(GL_MODELVIEW);
  glPushMatrix();
  glLoadIdentity();
  glColor3f(1.0F,1.0F,0.0F);
  glRasterPos2i(10,10);
  len=strlen(buf);
  for(i=0;i<len;i++)

  glutBitmapCharacter(GLUT_BITMAP_TIMES_ROMAN_24,buf[i]
  );
  glMatrixMode(GL_PROJECTION);
  glPopMatrix();
  glMatrixMode(GL_MODELVIEW);
  glPopMatrix();
  glPopAttrib();
  }
glutSwapBuffers();
}
```

Chapter 19. The Knight's Tour

The knight's tour example includes a lot of functionality, including rendering and moving pieces and the chessboard, 3D controls, user selection of materials, and chess move logic. The material selection dialog is shown below:

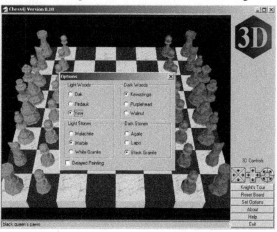

As the shape of the pieces is always the same, these are defined in data statements, such as the following:

```
typedef struct{short x1,y1,z1,x2,y2,z2,x3,y3,z3;}PIECE;

PIECE rook[]={
 { 1496,   229,     0, 1058,   229, 1058, 1579,    -5,
   0},
 { 1117,    -5, 1117, 1579,    -5,    0, 1058,   229,
   1058},
 { 1058,   229, 1058,    0,   229, 1496, 1117,    -5,
   1117},
 {    0,    -5, 1579, 1117,    -5, 1117,    0,   229,
   1496},
 {    0,   229, 1496,-1058,   229, 1058,    0,    -5,
   1579},
 {-1117,    -5, 1117,    0,    -5, 1579,-1058,   229,
   1058},
 {-1058,   229, 1058,-1496,   229,    0,-1117,    -5,
   1117},
 {-1579,    -5,    0,-1117,    -5, 1117,-1496,   229,
   0},
 {-1496,   229,    0,-1058,   229,-1058,-1579,    -5,
   0},
 {-1117,    -5,-1117,-1579,    -5,    0,-1058,   229,-
   1058},
 { etc,   etc,  etc,  etc,  etc,  etc,  etc,   etc,
   etc},
```

```
{32767,32767,32767,32767,32767,32767,32767,32767,3276
7}};
```

The last line containing 32767 indicates the end of data. Short integers are the smallest type and provide more than adequate resolution. The pieces are scaled as needed and assigned a texture by the following code:

```
typedef struct{
  float v[9];
  float n[3];
  DWORD color;
  }MESH;

MESH*Bishop;
MESH*King;
MESH*Knight;
MESH*Pawn;
MESH*Queen;
MESH*Rook;

MESH*InitializePiece(PIECE*p)
  {
  int i;
  MESH*m;
  for(i=0;p[i].x1!=32767;i++)
    continue;
  m=calloc(i+1,sizeof(MESH));
  for(i=0;p[i].x1!=32767;i++)
    {
    m[i].v[0]=p[i].x1/10000.;
    m[i].v[1]=p[i].y1/10000.;
    m[i].v[2]=p[i].z1/10000.;
    m[i].v[3]=p[i].x2/10000.;
    m[i].v[4]=p[i].y2/10000.;
    m[i].v[5]=p[i].z2/10000.;
    m[i].v[6]=p[i].x3/10000.;
    m[i].v[7]=p[i].y3/10000.;
    m[i].v[8]=p[i].z3/10000.;
    m[i].color=0x0000FF;
    }
  m[i].color=-1;
  return(m);
  }

void SetPiece(int i,MESH*mesh,DWORD*wood,int col,int
  row,int rotation)
  {
  Piece[i].mesh=mesh;
  Piece[i].name=Object[i];
```

```
  Piece[i].wood=wood;
  Piece[i].col=col;
  Piece[i].row=row;
  Piece[i].rotation=rotation;
  }

void InitializePieces()
  {
  Bishop=InitializePiece(bishop);
  King  =InitializePiece(king);
  Knight=InitializePiece(knight);
  Pawn  =InitializePiece(pawn);
  Queen =InitializePiece(queen);
  Rook  =InitializePiece(rook);
  SetPiece(0x00,Rook  ,&light_wood,0,0,  0);
  SetPiece(0x01,Knight,&light_wood,1,0,  0);
  SetPiece(0x02,Bishop,&light_wood,2,0,  0);
  SetPiece(0x03,Queen ,&light_wood,3,0,  0);
  SetPiece(0x04,King  ,&light_wood,4,0,  0);
  SetPiece(0x05,Bishop,&light_wood,5,0,  0);
  SetPiece(0x06,Knight,&light_wood,6,0,  0);
  SetPiece(0x07,Rook  ,&light_wood,7,0,  0);
  SetPiece(0x08,Pawn  ,&light_wood,0,1,  0);
  SetPiece(0x09,Pawn  ,&light_wood,1,1,  0);
  SetPiece(0x0A,Pawn  ,&light_wood,2,1,  0);
  SetPiece(0x0B,Pawn  ,&light_wood,3,1,  0);
  SetPiece(0x0C,Pawn  ,&light_wood,4,1,  0);
  SetPiece(0x0D,Pawn  ,&light_wood,5,1,  0);
  SetPiece(0x0E,Pawn  ,&light_wood,6,1,  0);
  SetPiece(0x0F,Pawn  ,&light_wood,7,1,  0);
  SetPiece(0x10,Rook  , &dark_wood,0,7,  0);
  SetPiece(0x11,Knight, &dark_wood,1,7,180);
  SetPiece(0x12,Bishop, &dark_wood,2,7,  0);
  SetPiece(0x13,Queen , &dark_wood,3,7,  0);
  SetPiece(0x14,King  , &dark_wood,4,7,  0);
  SetPiece(0x15,Bishop, &dark_wood,5,7,  0);
  SetPiece(0x16,Knight, &dark_wood,6,7,180);
  SetPiece(0x17,Rook  , &dark_wood,7,7,  0);
  SetPiece(0x18,Pawn  , &dark_wood,0,6,  0);
  SetPiece(0x19,Pawn  , &dark_wood,1,6,  0);
  SetPiece(0x1A,Pawn  , &dark_wood,2,6,  0);
  SetPiece(0x1B,Pawn  , &dark_wood,3,6,  0);
  SetPiece(0x1C,Pawn  , &dark_wood,4,6,  0);
  SetPiece(0x1D,Pawn  , &dark_wood,5,6,  0);
  SetPiece(0x1E,Pawn  , &dark_wood,6,6,  0);
  SetPiece(0x1F,Pawn  , &dark_wood,7,6,  0);
  }
```

The stone and wood textures are defined as resources:

```
Agate         BITMAP "agate.bmp"
```

```
BlackGranite BITMAP "blackgranite.bmp"
Lapis        BITMAP "lapis.bmp"
Malachite    BITMAP "malachite.bmp"
Marble       BITMAP "marble.bmp"
Oak          BITMAP "oak.bmp"
Pedauk       BITMAP "pedauk.bmp"
Purpleheart  BITMAP "purpleheart.bmp"
Walnut       BITMAP "walnut.bmp"
WhiteGranite BITMAP "whitegranite.bmp"
Yew          BITMAP "yew.bmp"
Kewazinga    BITMAP "kewazinga.bmp"
```

These are loaded by the following code:

```
DWORD LoadTexture(char*rname)
   {
   void*rLock;
   HGLOBAL rLoad;
   HRSRC rFind;
   BITMAPINFOHEADER*bm;
   if((rFind=FindResource(hInst,rname,RT_BITMAP))==NULL)
     Abort(__LINE__,"can't find resource %s\nWindows
     error code %li",rname,GetLastError());
   if((rLoad=LoadResource(hInst,rFind))==NULL)
     Abort(__LINE__,"can't load resource %s\nWindows
     error code %li",rname,GetLastError());
   if((rLock=LockResource(rLoad))==NULL)
     Abort(__LINE__,"can't lock resource %s\nWindows
     error code %li",rname,GetLastError());
   bm=(BITMAPINFOHEADER*)rLock;
   return(InitializeTexture(bm));
   }

void LoadTextures()
   {
   tAgate       =LoadTexture("Agate");
   tBlackGranite=LoadTexture("BlackGranite");
   tKewazinga   =LoadTexture("Kewazinga");
   tLapis       =LoadTexture("Lapis");
   tMalachite   =LoadTexture("Malachite");
   tMarble      =LoadTexture("Marble");
   tOak         =LoadTexture("Oak");
   tPedauk      =LoadTexture("Pedauk");
   tPurpleheart =LoadTexture("Purpleheart");
   tWalnut      =LoadTexture("Walnut");
   tWhiteGranite=LoadTexture("WhiteGranite");
   tYew         =LoadTexture("Yew");
   light_wood =tYew;
   dark_wood  =tKewazinga;;
   light_stone=tMarble;
   dark_stone =tBlackGranite;
```

```
    }
```

The board and pieces are rendered with the following code:

```
void PrepMesh(MESH*Mesh)
    {
    int i;
    VERTEX n,p,q;
    for(i=0;(Mesh[i].color&0x80000000)==0;i++)
      {
      p.x=Mesh[i].v[3]-Mesh[i].v[0];
      p.y=Mesh[i].v[4]-Mesh[i].v[1];
      p.z=Mesh[i].v[5]-Mesh[i].v[2];
      q.x=Mesh[i].v[6]-Mesh[i].v[0];
      q.y=Mesh[i].v[7]-Mesh[i].v[1];
      q.z=Mesh[i].v[8]-Mesh[i].v[2];
      n=CrossProduct(p,q);
      memcpy(Mesh[i].n,(float*)&n,3*sizeof(float));
      }
    }

void glMesh(MESH*Mesh,DWORD color,DWORD texture)
    {
    int i;
    if(fabs(Mesh[0].n[0])+fabs(Mesh[0].n[1])
      +fabs(Mesh[0].n[2])<FLT_EPSILON)
      PrepMesh(Mesh);
    if(texture)
      {
      glColor(WHITE);
      glEnable(GL_TEXTURE_2D);
      BindTexture(GL_TEXTURE_2D,texture);
      }
    else if(color)
      {
      glDisable(GL_TEXTURE_2D);
      glColor(color);
      }
    glBegin(GL_TRIANGLES);
    for(i=0;(Mesh[i].color&0x80000000)==0;i++)
      {
      glNormal3fv(Mesh[i].n);
      if(texture)
        {
        glVertexAndTex3fv(Mesh[i].v  ,texture);
        glVertexAndTex3fv(Mesh[i].v+3,texture);
        glVertexAndTex3fv(Mesh[i].v+6,texture);
        }
      else
        {
        if(color)
```

```
        glColor(color);
      else
        glColor(Mesh[i].color);
      glVertex3fv(Mesh[i].v);
      glVertex3fv(Mesh[i].v+3);
      glVertex3fv(Mesh[i].v+6);
      }
   }
  glEnd();
  if(texture)
    glDisable(GL_TEXTURE_2D);
  }

void SetView(int a,int b,int c,float s,float x,float
   y,float z)
  {
  View.a=a;
  View.b=b;
  View.c=c;
  View.s=s;
  View.x=x;
  View.y=y;
  View.z=z;
  }

void RenderTour()
  {
  int i,n;
  float a,r=0.0125,x1,x2,x3,x4,x5,x6,y=0.0125,
    z1,z2,z3,z4,z5,z6;
  glDisable(GL_TEXTURE_2D);
  glColor(0xFF0000);
  glBegin(GL_QUADS);
  glNormal3f(0.,1.,0.);
  x2=Brd[Tour[0].y];
  z2=Brd[Tour[0].x];
  n=min(64,pending_tour);
  for(i=1;i<n;i++)
    {
    x1=x2;
    z1=z2;
    x2=Brd[Tour[i].y];
    z2=Brd[Tour[i].x];
    a=atan2(z2-z1,x2-x1);
    x3=x1-r*sin(a);
    x4=x2-r*sin(a);
    x5=x1+r*sin(a);
    x6=x2+r*sin(a);
    z3=z1+r*cos(a);
```

```
    z4=z2+r*cos(a);
    z5=z1-r*cos(a);
    z6=z2-r*cos(a);
    glVertex3f(x3,y,z3);
    glVertex3f(x4,y,z4);
    glVertex3f(x6,y,z6);
    glVertex3f(x5,y,z5);
    }
  glEnd();
  }

void RenderBoard()
  {
  char board[]="??";
  int i,j,k;
  for(i=0;i<8;i++)
    {
    board[1]='1'+i;
    for(j=0;j<8;j++)
      {
      board[0]='A'+j;
      k=ObjectIndex(board);
      glStencilFunc(GL_ALWAYS,k,-1);
      if(k==selected)
        glHexahedron(Brd[i],-
  3./32.,Brd[j],3./8.,3./16.,3./8.,0xFF0000,0);
      else
        glHexahedron(Brd[i],-
  3./32.,Brd[j],3./8.,3./16.,3./8.,0,(i+j)%2?light_ston
    e:dark_stone);
      }
    }
  glStencilFunc(GL_ALWAYS,0,-1);
  }

void RenderPiece(MESH*piece,char*object,DWORD
    texture,float x,float z,float s,float b)
  {
  int k;
  k=ObjectIndex(object);
  glPushMatrix();
  glTranslatef(x,0,z);
  glScalef(s,s,s);
  glStencilFunc(GL_ALWAYS,k,-1);
  glRotatef(b,0,1,0);
  if(k==selected)
    glMesh(piece,0xFF0000,0);
  else
    glMesh(piece,0,texture);
```

```
glStencilFunc(GL_ALWAYS,0,-1);
glPopMatrix();
}

void RenderChess()
  {
  int i;

  ScaleTexture(2.);
  RenderBoard();

  if(light_wood==tOak)
    ScaleTexture(1.);
  else if(light_wood==tPedauk)
    ScaleTexture(2.);
  else
    ScaleTexture(25.);
  for(i=0;i<16;i++)
    if(Piece[i].row>=0)
      RenderPiece(Piece[i].mesh,Piece[i].name,
    *Piece[i].wood,Brd[Piece[i].row],Brd[Piece[i].col],
    0.75,Piece[i].rotation);

  if(dark_wood==tPurpleheart)
    ScaleTexture(5.);
  else
    ScaleTexture(2.);
  for(i=16;i<32;i++)
    if(Piece[i].row>=0)
      RenderPiece(Piece[i].mesh,Piece[i].name,
    *Piece[i].wood,Brd[Piece[i].row],Brd[Piece[i].col],
    0.75,Piece[i].rotation);

  if(pending_tour>0)
    RenderTour();
  }

void RenderScene()
  {
  float lp[4];

  if(!pDC)
    return;

  glClearDepth(1);
  glClearStencil(0);
  glClearColor(0,0,0,0);
  glClear(GL_COLOR_BUFFER_BIT|GL_DEPTH_BUFFER_BIT|
    GL_STENCIL_BUFFER_BIT);
```

```
glEnable(GL_DEPTH_TEST);
glDepthFunc(GL_LESS);
glFrontFace(GL_CCW);
glDisable(GL_CULL_FACE);
glCullFace(GL_BACK);

glEnable(GL_STENCIL_TEST);
glStencilOp(GL_KEEP,GL_KEEP,GL_REPLACE);
glStencilFunc(GL_ALWAYS,0,-1);

glShadeModel(GL_FLAT);
glDisable(GL_AUTO_NORMAL);
glEnable(GL_NORMALIZE);
glDisable(GL_BLEND);

glColorMaterial(GL_FRONT_AND_BACK,
  GL_AMBIENT_AND_DIFFUSE);
glEnable(GL_COLOR_MATERIAL);

glMatrixMode(GL_MODELVIEW);
glLoadIdentity();

if(fill_polygons)
  glPolygonMode(GL_FRONT_AND_BACK,GL_FILL);
else
  glPolygonMode(GL_FRONT_AND_BACK,GL_LINE);

glLightModeli(GL_LIGHT_MODEL_TWO_SIDE,FALSE);
glLightModeli(GL_LIGHT_MODEL_LOCAL_VIEWER,FALSE);
glLightModelfv(GL_LIGHT_MODEL_AMBIENT,
  floatColor(0x000000));

glLightfv(GL_LIGHT0,GL_AMBIENT ,floatColor(0x555555));
glLightfv(GL_LIGHT0,GL_DIFFUSE ,floatColor(0xAAAAAA));
glLightfv(GL_LIGHT0,GL_SPECULAR,floatColor(0x000000));
  lp[0]=sin(Light.a*M_PI/180)*cos(Light.b*M_PI/180);
  lp[2]=cos(Light.a*M_PI/180)*cos(Light.b*M_PI/180);
  lp[1]=sin(Light.b*M_PI/180);
  lp[3]=0;/* infinite distance to light source */
glLightfv(GL_LIGHT0,GL_POSITION,lp);
glEnable(GL_LIGHT0);
if(enable_lighting)
  glEnable(GL_LIGHTING);
else
  glDisable(GL_LIGHTING);

glColor(WHITE);
```

```
glRotatef(View.a,1,0,0);
glRotatef(View.b,0,1,0);
glRotatef(View.c,0,0,1);
glScalef(View.s,View.s,View.s);
glTranslatef(View.x,View.y,View.z);

RenderChess();

glFinish();
SwapBuffers(pDC);
}
```

The logic to solve the knight's walk is implemented with this very simple code (at least by chess standards):

```
int MoveOK(int x,int y)
{
if(x<0)
   return(0);
if(x>7)
   return(0);
if(y<0)
   return(0);
if(y>7)
   return(0);
if(board[y][x])
   return(0);
return(1);
}

int Moves(int x,int y)
{
int i,n;
for(n=i=0;i<8;i++)
   n+=MoveOK(x+move[i].x,y+move[i].y);
return(n);
}

int EndTour(int x1,int y1)
{
int i,m=0,n1,n2,x2,x3,y2,y3;
memset(board,0,sizeof(board));
board[y1][x1]=1;
Tour[0].x=x1;
Tour[0].y=y1;
while(1)
   {
   n1=9;
   for(i=0;i<8;i++)
      {
```

```
        x2=x1+move[i].x;
        y2=y1+move[i].y;
        if(!MoveOK(x2,y2))
          continue;
        if(m==62)
          {
          x3=x2;
          y3=y2;
          break;
          }
        n2=Moves(x2,y2);
        board[y2][x2]=0;
        if(n2<1||n2>=n1)
          continue;
        x3=x2;
        y3=y2;
        n1=n2;
        }
     if(n1==9&&m!=62)
        return(0);
     m++;
     x1=x3;
     y1=y3;
     board[y3][x3]=m+1;
     Tour[m].x=x3;
     Tour[m].y=y3;
     if(m==63)
        break;
     }
   return(m);
   }

void BeginTour(int s)
   {
   int x1,y1;
   x1=(int)(Object[s][0]-'A');
   y1=(int)(Object[s][1]-'1');
   if(EndTour(x1,y1))
     {
     for(pending_tour=1;pending_tour<=64;pending_tour++)
        {
        Piece[1].col=Tour[pending_tour-1].x;
        Piece[1].row=Tour[pending_tour-1].y;
        RePaint();
        }
     }
   else
     MessageBox(hMain,"knight's tour was not
     successful","algorithm failure",MB_APPLMODAL|MB_OK);
```

}

Chapter 20. Displaying Three-Dimensional Data

The Field3D example is different from any other contained in the archive as it correlates, interpolates, and displays three-dimensional data rather than some particular shape. Typical output is shown in the figure below:

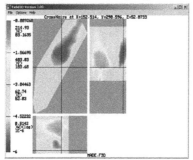

The large rectangle is the X-Y plane, the lower rectangle is the X-Z plane, and the right rectangle is the Y-Z plane. The crosshairs in all three rectangles are at the same location in three-dimensional space. The lower rectangle shows a vertical slice through the data where the horizontal black line passes through it. The right rectangle shows a vertical slice through the data where the vertical black line passes through it. This figure printed and folded along the edges to illustrate the relationship between the three views is shown below:

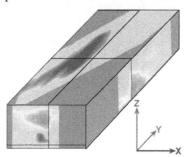

There are several two- and three-dimensional sets provided with this example (*.DAT) as well as pre-compiled fields (*.F3D). There are also batch files (_make_*.bat) that illustrate the various command line options and re-compile the fields.

This following example shows topography with additional information overlaid. The elevations are color coded from blue (sea level) to red (250 feet).

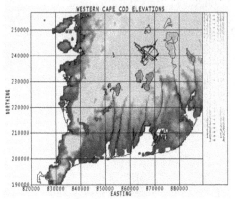

The same topography in 3D with considerable vertical exaggeration:

Field3D will also write out 2D and 3D table files (*.TB2 and *.TB3) that contain the results of interpolation in a convenient tabular format. Such a table was used to construct the previous two graphics.

Appendix A: Example Details & Setup

There are over fifty fully functional examples included in the online archive:

https://www.dudleybenton.altervista.org/software/3D Rendering/3D_Rendering_in_Windows.zip

Each one is complete and will unpack into a separate folder. The examples have been precompiled and will run on any version of Windows®. There is also an Excel® spreadsheet listing the examples in the top-level folder.

Name/Folder	Engine	Extra	Colors	Level	Anim.	Features
Accnot	OpenGL		24-bit	1	0	simple example using built-in shapes
Alpha3D	OpenGL	GLAUX	24-bit	4	0	illustrates intermixing of opaque and alpha blending; also mouse click input
Atlantis	OpenGL	GLUT	24-bit	3	1	animation objects (fish swimming around)
Blender	OpenGL	GLUT	24-bit	3	1	fade, animations, text (with anti-aliasing)
Blue Pony	OpenGL	Mesa	24-bit	3	2	animation, bitmap images, extrusion of parts (2D to 3D)
Bounce	OpenGL	Mesa	24-bit	3	1	bouncing checkered sphere
Chess	OpenGL	GLUT	24-bit	3	1	animation, chess pieces, chess board movements
Cube Map	OpenGL	Mesa	24-bit	2	1	rotating sphere inside rotating cube with checkerboard textures
Dino Ball	OpenGL	GLUT	24-bit	3	1	extrusion (2D to 3D), click and drag to rotate
Dino Draw	OpenGL	GLUT	24-bit	3	1	extrusion (2D to 3D), animation, click to activate
Dino Shade	OpenGL	GLUT	24-bit	4	1	extrusion (2D to 3D), animation, shadows, reflections
Dino Spin	OpenGL	GLUT	24-bit	3	1	extrusion (2D to 3D), animation, click to activate, text
DOF not	OpenGL	GLAUX	24-bit	2	0	depth-of-field illustration with 5 teapots
Earth & Moon	OpenGL	Mesa	24-bit	2	1	rotating spheres covered with photographs

Field3D	WinAPI	none	N/A	4	3	create 3D fields from data and display in slices
flange	WinAPI	none	24-bit	2	1	simple sort and paint back to front
Fog	OpenGL	GLAUX	24-bit	2	0	illustrates 3 types of fog; also mouse click input
Gears	OpenGL	Mesa	24-bit	3	1	three rotating gears
GearTrain	OpenGL	Mesa	24-bit	3	1	more complex gears
GL Puzzle	OpenGL	GLUT	24-bit	2	1	buttons, mouse menus, animation
Ideas	OpenGL	GLUT	24-bit	4	1	animation, shapes interacting with planes, lighting, changing viewpoint
IsoSurf	OpenGL	Mesa	24-bit	3	0	arbitrary surface, lighting, rotation, keyboard input
Knight's Tour	OpenGL	none	24-bit	4	3	animation, textures, controls, logic, interaction
Long Ago	WinAPI	none	N/A	1	1	familiar scrolling yellow text, star field simulation, Star Wars Theme
Lorenz	OpenGL	GLUT	24-bit	2	1	animated spheres and lines
Material	OpenGL	GLAUX	24-bit	2	0	12 spheres with different surface/light interaction
Morph3D	OpenGL	Mesa	24-bit	2	2	transforming geometric shapes, animation, keyboard input
Move Light	OpenGL	GLAUX	24-bit	2	3	click the mouse to move the light source around a torus
Occlude	OpenGL	Mesa	24-bit	2	1	occlusion test
Olympic Rings	OpenGL	none	24-bit	2	1	animated toruses forming olympic logo
Origami	OpenGL	GLUT	24-bit	3	2	continuous shape changing while animating with rotating viewpoint
Planet Up	OpenGL	GLAUX	24-bit	1	1	Earth & Moon as wireframe spheres; press arrow keys to rotate/orbit
Point Burst	OpenGL	GLUT	24-bit	3	1	little spheres bursting forth and bouncing into view
Reflect	OpenGL	Mesa	24-bit	3	1	rotating reflective torus shows an image
Reflect Dino	OpenGL	GLUT	24-bit	4	1	extrusion (2D to 3D), animation, reflections

Reflect2	OpenGL	Mesa	24-bit	3	1	rotating cylinder and cone produce reflection
Roller Coaster	OpenGL	GLUT	24-bit	4	1	animation, complex object building, changing viewpoint (following coaster)
scclrlt	OpenGL	GLAUX	24-bit	1	0	color light source with stock shapes
scene	OpenGL	GLAUX	24-bit	1	0	white light source with stock shapes
Shapes	OpenGL	none	24-bit	3	3	create and display various geometric shapes using OpenGL
Sky Fly	OpenGL	GLUT	24-bit	4	3	interactive fly over with terrain and clouds
SpinCube	WinAPI	none	N/A	2	1	rotating cube screen saver displays BMP, GIF, or JPG
Stonehenge1	OpenGL	GLAUX	24-bit	3	3	fog, rain, lighting, animated tour
Stonehenge2	OpenGL	none	24-bit	3	3	more advanced rendering and controls
Stonehenge3	My3D	none	24-bit	4	3	fog, lighting, rotations, textures, buttons
surface	WinAPI		24-bit	2	2	simple sort and paint; use keys to rotate and zoom
Tea Amb	OpenGL	GLAUX	24-bit	1	0	three options for ambient lighting
Teapot	OpenGL	Mesa	24-bit	3	0	rotating teapot with shadow, moving light, and textures
Teapots	OpenGL	none	24-bit	2	0	surface effects (shiny, dull, plastic, metallic, etc.)
TexGen	OpenGL	GLAUX	24-bit	2	0	illustrates how to generate and apply a texture
Tprim	OpenGL	GLAUX	24-bit	1	0	illustrates drawing primitives (lines, polygons, etc.)
tselect	OpenGL	GLAUX	24-bit	2	3	illustrates how to select objects with the mouse
View3D	My3D	none	8-bit	4	3	automatic capture to GIF, import AutoCAD 3D Studio files
View3DS	OpenGL	none	24-bit	4	3	load 3D Studio models and display them using OpenGL
VRML View	WinAPI	none	24-bit	2	2	reads and displays VRML files

Win3D	Win3D	none	N/A	2	1	hidden line/surface removal; interference; 3D font; no source code

Note1: GLAX is the OpenGL auxiliary library

Note2: GLUT is the OpenGL utilities library

Note3: Mesa is Brian Paul's additions to OpenGL

Note4: My3D is rendering engine I developed, completely independent of OpenGL

Note5: All copyright notices are in the respective source code files.

Unpack the archive into a folder of your choice. You may need to copy the include files (*.h) from the gl folder into the include folder associated with your compiler and the library files (*.lib) into the lib folder. There are three different versions of these files in separate subfolders by year of issue. I have put the most common at the top level. You will know immediately whether you need to copy these files, as the compiler will display a message that it can't find one or more of the include files and exit.

I build everything from a command prompt (which, incidentally is not a DOS box). This may or may not work with what you use to write code, presumably some sort of text editor. I don't recommend Visual Studio®. It's very expensive and completely unnecessary. Each of the examples is in a separate folder, containing everything you need to build it. There is a small batch file, _compile.bat, in each folder to compile that example. These batch files depend on your having already set up a folder containing the Microsoft® compiler (for details see Appendix B).

Appendix B: C Compilers

If you don't have a C compiler, I suggest either Digital Mars® or Microsoft®. The former can be downloaded free from:

http://www.digitalmars.com/

The Microsoft® C compiler is also available free of charge. The thing that costs so much is the Visual Studio® Interactive Development Environment, which is completely unnecessary and extremely annoying. Simply download and install the W7.1 SDK and DDK from the Microsoft@ Download Center:

https://www.microsoft.com/en-us/download

You may have to convert the DDK from an ISO to something else. You can simply burn it onto a DVD or a memory stick. Either way you'll need software for that purpose. After you install the two kits, combine the bin, include, and lib folders and put them in a folder called C:\VC32. There will be several folders with similar names. The folders you need will have x86 in them, even if you have an x64 machine.

I do not recommend the Gnu® compiler, gcc, as it was developed specifically for Linux®. While it does run on Windows® and may produce viable executables, it is very quirky, assumes all sorts of things that aren't ANSI (as far as I can tell), and is nothing but trouble. Considering that both the Digital Mars® and Microsoft® compilers are available free, there is no reason to use gcc.

Appendix C: Pixel Formats

The term pixel format is tossed about in OpenGL® literature as if it were intuitive or had meaning in a broad context. Of course, it doesn't, particularly in the context of Windows® programming. The Windows® APIs use completely different terminology and the documentation doesn't mention pixel formats. While the terminology is unfamiliar, the concepts are not.

In order to paint anything in Windows® you must have a handle to a device context. When this device context is in memory, it's called a compatible device context. In order to paint on the display without flicker, you must first build the image in memory and then BitBlt it onto the display. Color images in memory are called DIB sections. You must select the DIB section into the memory device context. The combination of a memory device context and a DIB section (plus a few other things, including a Z-buffer) is called a pixel format.

OpenGL® works with pixel formats. You can see what pixel formats are available by calling DescribePixelFormat(). You select the one you want by calling SetPixelFormat(). You prepare it for use with OpenGL® by calling wglCreateContext() and one from many by calling wglMakeCurrent(). When it comes time to paint it onto the display, you call SwapBuffers(), which hopefully just paints them rather than swapping them.

Pixel formats, along with these virtually undocumented API calls, are defined in wingdi.h and ntgdi.h. Other than facilitating OpenGL® rendering, it's not clear why these even exist in the Windows® context or why they are linked in gdi32.lib and implemented in gdi32.dll. Whatever the reason, this is what they are and you're going to need them to do anything with OpenGL®.

You must get a pixel format before doing anything with OpenGL®. You don't get to request a particular pixel format; rather, you must select one from a list that will work for you intend to do. You get a list of available formats by calling DescribePixelFormat(). The following is a typical list of such formats:

index	OpenGL	double buffer	RGBA	need palette	system palette	color bits	depth bits	stencil bits	generic	accele-rated	score	stencil score
1	1	0	1	0	0	32	24	0	0	0	0	0
2	1	0	1	0	0	32	24	0	0	0	0	0
3	1	0	1	0	0	32	24	8	0	1	0	0
4	1	0	1	0	0	32	24	8	0	0	0	0
5	1	0	1	0	0	32	0	0	0	0	0	0
6	1	0	1	0	0	32	0	0	0	0	0	0
7	1	1	1	0	0	32	24	0	0	0	80	0
8	1	1	1	0	0	32	24	0	0	0	80	0
9	1	1	1	0	0	32	24	8	0	1	88	88
10	1	1	1	0	0	32	24	8	0	0	80	80
11	1	1	1	0	0	32	0	0	0	0	64	0
12	1	1	1	0	0	32	0	0	0	0	64	0
13	1	1	1	0	0	32	24	0	0	0	80	0
14	1	1	1	0	0	32	24	0	0	0	80	0
19	0	1	1	0	0	32	24	0	0	0	0	0
90	0	1	1	0	0	32	24	8	0	0	0	0
91	1	0	1	0	0	32	32	8	1	1	0	0
92	1	0	1	0	0	32	16	8	1	0	0	0
93	1	1	1	0	0	32	32	8	1	1	90	90
94	1	1	1	0	0	32	16	8	1	0	82	82
95	1	0	1	0	0	32	32	8	1	1	0	0
96	1	0	1	0	0	32	16	8	1	0	0	0
97	1	1	1	0	0	32	32	8	1	0	82	82
98	1	1	1	0	0	32	16	8	1	0	82	82
99	1	0	0	0	0	32	32	8	1	1	0	0
100	1	0	0	0	0	32	16	8	1	0	0	0
101	1	1	0	0	0	32	32	8	1	1	0	0
102	1	1	0	0	0	32	16	8	1	0	0	0
105	1	0	1	0	0	24	32	8	1	0	0	0
106	1	0	1	0	0	24	16	8	1	0	0	0
107	1	0	0	0	0	24	32	8	1	0	0	0
108	1	0	0	0	0	24	16	8	1	0	0	0
111	1	0	1	0	0	16	32	8	1	0	0	0
112	1	0	1	0	0	16	16	8	1	0	0	0
113	1	0	0	0	0	16	32	8	1	0	0	0
114	1	0	0	0	0	16	16	8	1	0	0	0
125	1	0	0	1	1	4	32	8	1	0	0	0
126	1	0	0	1	1	4	16	8	1	0	0	0

This table has been abbreviated for space, but still illustrates the selection process you must go through in order to select an appropriate pixel format. First of all, some of the available formats don't even support OpenGL®. These are eliminated immediately. Ones that don't support double buffering or require a palette can also be eliminated. OpenGL® depends on RGBA, so formats that don't support this can also be eliminated. The color depth should be at least 24 and will paint faster if this matches the depth of the display device context.

The depth bits are used for the Z-buffer and must be at least 16. Generic doesn't matter. Accelerated may draw faster, but is not always available, depending on hardware and drivers. If you want to use stenciling, that can be included in the criteria. I calculate a score for each and pick the one with the highest score. If none of the available formats score above zero, exit the program. The following code snippet implements this selection process:

```
HDC GetBestPixelFormat(HDC hDC,int stencil)
 {
int i,j,n,s,sx;
PIXELFORMATDESCRIPTOR pfd;
if((n=DescribePixelFormat(hDC,1,0,NULL))<1)
return(NULL);
j=sx=-1;
for(i=1;i<=n;i++)
 {
DescribePixelFormat(hDC,i,
   sizeof(PIXELFORMATDESCRIPTOR),&pfd);
if(!(pfd.dwFlags&PFD_SUPPORT_OPENGL))
 continue;
if(!(pfd.dwFlags&PFD_DOUBLEBUFFER))
 continue;
if(pfd.iPixelType!=PFD_TYPE_RGBA)
 continue;
if(pfd.dwFlags&PFD_NEED_PALETTE)
 continue;
if(pfd.dwFlags&PFD_NEED_SYSTEM_PALETTE)
 continue;
if(pfd.cColorBits<24)
 continue;
if(pfd.cDepthBits<16)
 continue;
if((1<<pfd.cStencilBits)<stencil)
 continue;
s=pfd.cDepthBits/16;
if(pfd.dwFlags&PFD_GENERIC_ACCELERATED)
 s+=2;
if(pfd.cColorBits==GetDeviceCaps(hDC,BITSPIXEL))
 s+=8;
else if(pfd.cColorBits>=24)
 s+=4;
```

```
if(s<sx)
 continue;
sx=s;
j=i;
}
if(j<0)
return(NULL);
DescribePixelFormat(hDC,j,
  sizeof(PIXELFORMATDESCRIPTOR),&pfd);
if(!SetPixelFormat(hDC,j,&pfd))
return(NULL);
return(hDC);
}
```

Appendix D: GLUT & Windows

The OpenGL® Utilities Library, or GLUT, is a convenient addition to the basic library, but it there are subtleties that you need to know when using this on the Windows® operating system. Windows® applications work with handles and device contexts, but the GLUT functions do not provide these. If you want to build a fully functional Windows® application, you will need at least some of these essentials.

If you use glutInit(), glutInitWindowPosition(), glutInitWindowSize(), and glutMainLoop() to begin an application, as is the case in all of the Mesa examples, you will first need the handle to the instance. There are two ways of getting this: 1) as the first argument in WinMain(), or 2) the API function GetModuleHandle().

```
HINSTANCE hInst;
int WINAPI WinMain(HINSTANCE hInstance,HINSTANCE
    hPrev,char*lpszLine,int nShow)
{
  hInst=hInstance;
```

or

```
hInst=GetModuleHandle(NULL);
```

The main procedure of a Windows® application is supposed to be WinMain(), not main(), although the latter will work and give you an extraneous console window. WinMain() does not come with the command line arguments, but these are available through global variables:

```
extern int __argc;
extern char**__argv;
extern char**_environ;
```

GLUT creates a top-level window, but you need this to be a child window within the structure of your program. To accomplish this, you must first let GLUT create its window. That way it will be the only active window. Use the GetActiveWindow() API call to get the handle to the GLUT window. Then create your own top-level window using CreateWindow(). Finally, use the API function SetParent() to make the GLUT window a child of your window.

You may also need the device context of the GLUT window. Use the API functions GetDC() followed by ReleaseDC() to get this device context. You must release it so that OpenGL® can work with it. Do not use the API functions CreateDC() and DeleteDC(), as this device context has already been created.

If you need a handle to the bitmap in the device context created by GLUT, first create a compatible bitmap from the device context. Then select this into the device context using the API function SelectObject(). This function will return the handle of the bitmap that was selected into the device context. Select it back into the device context and then destroy the compatible bitmap. This process is illustrated in the following code snippet:

```
HBITMAP GetGlutBitmap(HDC glutDC)
 {
 HBITMAP compHB,glutHB;
 compHB=CreateCompatibleBitmap(glutDC,32,32);
 glutHB=SelectObject(glutDC,compHB);
 SelectObject(glutDC,glutHB)
 DeleteObject(compHB);
 return(glutHB);
 }
```

Appendix E: Long Ago...

The long ago example illustrates how to draw text that appears to be moving away from you as well as stars that you appear to be approaching. It also illustrates how to play a WAV file. Drawing the scrolling text without flicker requires two device contexts: 1) the display (or desktop) that you're painting onto, 2) the context where you draw stars and text. To eliminate flicker, use the BitBlt() API function to paint the final result onto the desktop.

There are two versions of this example. The first is 8 bits/pixel color so that each pixel is defined by a single byte. This facilitates distorting the text. The second example is 24 bits/pixel color and uses StretchBlt() to distort the text. The first illustrates byte-by-byte bitmap manipulations and the second illustrates the use of multiple device contexts and the GdiTransparentBlt() function to copy the text onto the stars.

Appendix F: Spinning Cube

The spinning cube demo was part of the earliest Microsoft® Software Developer Kits. The problem is, it was very poorly written and didn't work properly. It also would only read BMP files. I have completely rewritten it and added GIF and JPG formats. If you need functions to load, manipulate, and change any of these three image formats, you will find them in the Spin Cube folder.

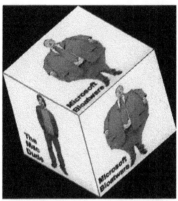

This example uses a memory device context to build the image and BitBlt() to paint. It also keeps track of the part of the display that is changed, so that the minimum area is repainted. It uses the PlgBlt() to shear the images into parallelograms corresponding to the cube.

The setup also doesn't work in the SDK example. It's a little tricky to get a screen saver to run inside the preview window, as illustrated below. It's also necessary to set options and make adjustments, which requires a dialog and message processing. All of this is included in the revised edition of Spin Cube.

Appendix G: Using the Stencil Buffer to Identify Objects

Another use for stenciling in OpenGL® is that of object identification. If you set the stencil value to the index of each object before it is drawn, the stencil buffer will contain the index of the top most object for each pixel. You can use the row and column corresponding to the crosshairs of the cursor to get the index of the object visible at that location and then use this index to look up the name of the object in a list. You can then display the name of the object under the cursor. Three examples illustrate the use of this method: knight's tour, Stonehenge 2, and View3DS. These examples also show where to put the message processing needed to receive the cursor movements and how to translate these into coordinates within the graphics window of your application.

Appendix H: Random Numbers

Random numbers are often used in rendering to create surfaces and simulated textures. The standard library (stdio.h) uses the following algorithm to produce random numbers:

```
short int rand(void)
    {
    static unsigned long int r=1;
    r=r*1103515245UL+12345UL;
    return((unsigned short int)(r/0x10000UL)&0x7FFF);
    }
```

Park & Miller[7] suggest the following simple algorithm:

```
short int random()
    {
    static long int seed=1;
    seed=(16807*seed)%2147483647;
    return(seed/2147483647);
    }
```

Marsaglia[8] has provided the following, considerably more complicated algorithm:

```
#define PHI 0x9e3779b9

static uint32_t Q[4096],c=362436;

void init_rand(uint32_t x)
    {
    int i;
    Q[0]=x;
    Q[1]=x+PHI;
    Q[2]=x+PHI+PHI;
    for(i=3;i<4096;i++)
        Q[i]=Q[i-3]^Q[i-2]^PHI^i;
    }

uint32_t rand_cmwc(void)
    {
    uint64_t t,a=18782LL;
    static uint32_t i=4095;
    uint32_t x,r=0xfffffffe;
    i=(i+1)&4095;
    t=a*Q[i]+c;
    c=(t>>32);
```

---

[7] "Random Number Generators: Good Ones Are Hard to Find," Park, S. K, and Miller, K. W., *Communications of the ACM*, Volume 31 Issue 10, Oct. 1988, pp. 1192-1201.

[8] Marsaglia, G. "Random Number Generators", *Journal of Modern Applied Statistical Methods*, Vol. 2., 2003.

```
x=t+c;
if(x<c)
  {
  x++;
  c++;
  }
Q[i]=r-x;
return(Q[i]);
}
```

The Sky Fly example includes an advanced random number generator (random.c), developed at the University of California, Berkley. There are numerous less complicated random number generators that could be used with fully adequate results, which is why I replaced the Berkley algorithm with the following, much simpler one:

```
long random()
  {
union{short s[2];long l}u;
u.s[0]=rand();
u.s[1]=rand();
return(u.l);
}
```

This same technique could be used to further randomize the result:

```
long random()
  {
int i;
union{BYTE b[4];long l;}u;
for(i=0;i<4;i++)
  u.b[i]=(BYTE)(((unsigned)rand())%256);
return(u.l);
}
```

These algorithms produce uniformly distributed random numbers, rather than normally distributed (a.k.a., Gaussian) random numbers. The difference between these two is illustrated in the following figure:

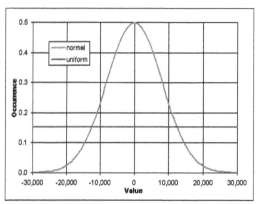

There are several algorithms for converting uniformly distributed random numbers into normally distributed random numbers. The simplest is listed below for both integer and real numbers:

```
short int rnorm()
  {
  short int i;
  long l;
  for(l=i=0;i<12;i++)
    l+=rand();
  i=(short int)(l/12);
  return(i);
  }
double rdist(double avg,double std)
  {
  int i;
  double r;
  r=0.;
  for(i=0;i<12;i++)
    r+=rand()/32767.;
  return(avg+std*(r/6.-1.));
  }
```

Appendix I. Win3D by Leendert Ammeraal

This tool is an oldie, but a goodie. It's also free! I have included it in the archive as-is for your use. While you don't get the source code for this very useful tool, it provides an excellent illustration of several important concepts and can be used to create, import, and export 3D models. It recognizes several different file formats, including DXF. The following description of Win3D is provided in the help file:

> If you are interested in the mathematical principles and programming aspects on which this program is based, you can use the following books for further reference. They are by Leendert Ammeraal and published by John Wiley, Chichester, England. Some programs (in their executable form) and some data files discussed in the first two of these books are also on the Win3D distribution disk:
>
> *Programming Principles in Computer Graphics, 2nd Ed. (1992)
> *Interactive 3D Computer Graphics (1988)
> *Windows Wisdom for C and C++ Programmers (1993)
> *Programs and Data Structures in C, 2nd Ed. (1992)
> *C for Programmers, 2nd Ed. (1991)
> *C++ for Programmers (1991)
> *Graphics Programming in Turbo C (1989)
>
> If you have any comments on Win3D or on the above books, please write to the publisher (at the address given by File | About Win3D...), or to the author: Leendert Ammeraal, Reigerlaan 4, 1241 ED Kortenhoef, The Netherlands.

Perhaps the two most interesting aspects of Win3D are the implementation of hidden lines/surfaces and intersections between objects. Hidden lines are illustrated in the following figure:

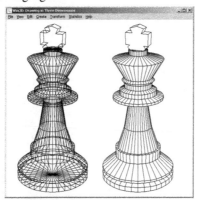

The "solid" view of this same chess king is shown in the following figure:

117

The facility of Win3D to find the intersection between two objects is illustrated in this next figure:

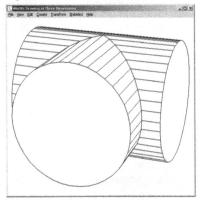

The solid rendering is shown below:

also by D. James Benton

3D Articulation: Using OpenGL, ISBN-9798596362480, Amazon, 2021 (book 3 in the 3D series).

3D Models in Motion Using OpenGL, ISBN-9798652987701, Amazon, 2020 (book 2 in the 3D series.

A Synergy of Short Stories: The whole may be greater than the sum of the parts, ISBN-9781520340319, Amazon, 2016.

Azeotropes: Behavior and Application, ISBN-9798609748997, Amazon, 2020.

bat-Elohim: Book 3 in the Little Star Trilogy, ISBN-9781686148682, Amazon, 2019.

Boilers: Performance and Testing, ISBN: 9798789062517, Amazon 2021.

Combined 3D Rendering Series: 3D Rendering in Windows®, 3D Models in Motion, and 3D Articulation, ISBN-9798484417032, Amazon, 2021.

Complex Variables: Practical Applications, ISBN-9781794250437, Amazon, 2019.

Compression & Encryption: Algorithms & Software, ISBN-9781081008826, Amazon, 2019.

Computational Fluid Dynamics: an Overview of Methods, ISBN-9781672393775, Amazon, 2019.

Computer Simulation of Power Systems: Programming Strategies and Practical Examples, ISBN-9781696218184, Amazon, 2019.

Contaminant Transport: A Numerical Approach, ISBN-9798461733216, Amazon, 2021.

CPUnleashed! Tapping Processor Speed, ISBN-9798421420361, Amazon, 2022.

Curve-Fitting: The Science and Art of Approximation, ISBN-9781520339542, Amazon, 2016.

Death by Tie: It was the best of ties. It was the worst of ties. It's what got him killed., ISBN-9798398745931, Amazon, 2023.

Differential Equations: Numerical Methods for Solving, ISBN-9781983004162, Amazon, 2018.

Equations of State: A Graphical Comparison, ISBN-9798843139520, Amazon, 2022.

Evaporative Cooling: The Science of Beating the Heat, ISBN-9781520913346, Amazon, 2017.

Forecasting: Extrapolation and Projection, ISBN-9798394019494, Amazon 2023.

Heat Engines: Thermodynamics, Cycles, & Performance Curves, ISBN-9798486886836, Amazon, 2021.

Heat Exchangers: Performance Prediction & Evaluation, ISBN-9781973589327, Amazon, 2017.

Heat Recovery Steam Generators: Thermal Design and Testing, ISBN-9781691029365, Amazon, 2019.

Heat Transfer: Heat Exchangers, Heat Recovery Steam Generators, & Cooling Towers, ISBN-9798487417831, Amazon, 2021.

Heat Transfer Examples: Practical Problems Solved, ISBN-9798390610763, Amazon, 2023.

The Kick-Start Murders: Visualize revenge, ISBN-9798759083375, Amazon, 2021.

Jamie2: Innocence is easily lost and cannot be restored, ISBN-9781520339375, Amazon, 2016-18.

Kyle Cooper Mysteries: Kick Start, Monte Carlo, and Waterfront Murders, ISBN-9798829365943, Amazon, 2022.

The Last Seraph: Sequel to Little Star, ISBN-9781726802253, Amazon, 2018.

Little Star: God doesn't do things the way we expect Him to. He's better than that! ISBN-9781520338903, Amazon, 2015-17.

Living Math: Seeing mathematics in every day life (and appreciating it more too), ISBN-9781520336992, Amazon, 2016.

Lost Cause: If only history could be changed..., ISBN-9781521173770, Amazon, 2017.

Mass Transfer: Diffusion & Convection, ISBN-9798702403106, Amazon, 2021.

Mill Town Destiny: The Hand of Providence brought them together to rescue the mill, the town, and each other, ISBN-9781520864679, Amazon, 2017.

Monte Carlo Murders: Who Killed Who and Why, ISBN-9798829341848, Amazon, 2022.

Monte Carlo Simulation: The Art of Random Process Characterization, ISBN-9781980577874, Amazon, 2018.

Nonlinear Equations: Numerical Methods for Solving, ISBN-9781717767318, Amazon, 2018.

Numerical Calculus: Differentiation and Integration, ISBN-9781980680901, Amazon, 2018.

Numerical Methods: Nonlinear Equations, Numerical Calculus, & Differential Equations, ISBN-9798486246845, Amazon, 2021.

Orthogonal Functions: The Many Uses of, ISBN-9781719876162, Amazon, 2018.

Overwhelming Evidence: A Pilgrimage, ISBN-9798515642211, Amazon, 2021.

Particle Tracking: Computational Strategies and Diverse Examples, ISBN-9781692512651, Amazon, 2019.

Plumes: Delineation & Transport, ISBN-9781702292771, Amazon, 2019.

Power Plant Performance Curves: for Testing and Dispatch, ISBN-9798640192698, Amazon, 2020.

Practical Linear Algebra: Principles & Software, ISBN-9798860910584, Amazon, 2023.

Props, Fans, & Pumps: Design & Performance, ISBN-9798645391195, Amazon, 2020.

Remediation: Contaminant Transport, Particle Tracking, & Plumes, ISBN-9798485651190, Amazon, 2021.

ROFL: Rolling on the Floor Laughing, ISBN-9781973300007, Amazon, 2017.

Seminole Rain: You don't choose destiny. It chooses you, ISBN-9798668502196, Amazon, 2020.

Septillionth: 1 in 10^{24}, ISBN-9798410762472, Amazon, 2022.

Software Development: Targeted Applications, ISBN-9798850653989, Amazon, 2023.

Software Recipes: Proven Tools, ISBN-9798815229556, Amazon, 2022.

Steam 2020: to 150 GPa and 6000 K, ISBN-9798634643830, Amazon, 2020.

Thermochemical Reactions: Numerical Solutions, ISBN-9781073417872, Amazon, 2019.

Thermodynamic and Transport Properties of Fluids, ISBN-9781092120845, Amazon, 2019.

Thermodynamic Cycles: Effective Modeling Strategies for Software Development, ISBN-9781070934372, Amazon, 2019.

Thermodynamics - Theory & Practice: The science of energy and power, ISBN-9781520339795, Amazon, 2016.

Version-Independent Programming: Code Development Guidelines for the Windows® Operating System, ISBN-9781520339146, Amazon, 2016.

The Waterfront Murders: As you sow, so shall you reap, ISBN-9798611314500, Amazon, 2020.

Weather Data: Where To Get It and How To Process It, ISBN-9798868037894, Amazon, 2023.